# Acknowledgements

**D**ee and I would like to thank all of you who have been involved. We hope you enjoy reading our book as much as we have enjoyed producing it. Of course there would be no home cooking book at all if those associated with the three charities had not sent in all those interesting and delicious recipes. Thank you all!

Ian adapted and standardised the recipes so the weights and measures are uniform. We hope the changes have not altered the flavour of your dishes too much. Not all the recipes sent in to us are in the book. There were some duplicates and we held unwaveringly to the rule that the first one sent to us is the recipe and the dish we included. Also we tried to keep a balance (not always easy in this type of cookery book); for example we were inundated with great chicken recipes so we needed to hold back on a few. Finally it has to be said that some recipes where sent in just too late. May be there will be a follow on book?

There are some people we would like to mention by name. At WSBPS, their fund raiser Lynne Sedgewick was a great enthusiast for the book and was always ready with a coffee when things were going less than well. Sue Hadley, their Chairperson, helped considerably to push the project forward. Jenny Borely was always supportive (do try her chutney which is legendary). At the Foundation Simon Harding was a great coordinator and spurred us on; Tom Southern and Heather Sutton worked tirelessly getting things going from their end. We would like to thank Jim Moran for endorsing this project at Bradbury Fields even all though he admits to having little interest in cooking. In addition Margaret Guppy provided all their recipes.

Books only come to life because of the industry of the project team. Our project "midwives" were Dave Coffey and Simon Castell. We thank them both for all their ingenuity and skill but also for their generosity particularly with respect to the time they gave to the project.

**Ian and Dee Grierson**

An Eye For Good Food

# an eye for good food

## Recipes from 3 Eye Charities

Ian Grierson BSc PhD FIBiol FRCPath.
with Dee Grierson

**WSBPS** — Wirral Society of the Blind and Partially Sighted. Est. 1989

The Foundation for the Prevention of Blindness
St Paul's Eye Appeal
Registered Charity No: 1047988

Bradbury Fields
services for blind and partially sighted people
Registered Charity number 222798

ISBN: 978-0-9564297-0-4

# Contents

9     A tale of three eye charities

10     WSBPS

12     The Foundation for the Prevention of Blindness

14     Bradbury Fields

16     Homage to home cooking

19     Soups & Starters

39     Salads

49     Main Courses

85     Desserts

93     Chutneys & Drinks

**Published by:**
EAST PARK COMMUNICATIONS Ltd.
Old School House,
Liscard Road, Liscard,
Wallasey, Merseyside CH44 5TN
Tel: 0151 691 4925
simon@epc.gb.com
www.epc.gb.com

**ISBN:**
978-0-9564297-0-4

**Designed by:**
East Park Studio

© East Park Communications Ltd.
November 2009

**Media No.**
1045

**Legal Notice**
None of the editorial or photographs may be reproduced without prior written permission from the publishers.

The International Glaucoma Association would like to point out that all editorial comment and articles are the responsibility of the originators and may or may not reflect the opinions of The International Glaucoma Association.

All information contained herein is correct at time of going to press.

An Eye For Good Food

An Eye For Good Food

# A Tale of Three Eye Charities

I enjoy compiling recipe books and it has gone from being a harmless hobby to an all consuming obsession – please forgive the pun! As a way of exorcising this particular demon I have agreed to do another book but this time it is for 3 Merseyside Eye charities. To illustrate how sad I have become I admit that I started compiling the recipe book at Easter on holiday in Spain. As I write these words I am fully aware that it is raining back home but here there are cloudless skies and the children and Dee (my co-compiler) are outside by a swimming pool taking full advantage of the excellent facilities. It is a grim addiction to prefer struggling with a laptop rather than relaxing with a Sangria however our 3 charities are extremely important ones and I am sure most of you will know of them but it is only polite to introduce them to you.

The first of the charities is the **Wirral Society of the Blind and Partially Sighted**. A key word in the Society title is that it is "of" not "for". The founders of the Society were rightly at pains to emphasise that this is a society made "of" the blind and partially sighted and no one made it "for" them! In fact it is with the WSBPS that my interest in publishing recipes began. I have had the honour of being their patron for many years and Dee and I have enjoyed the friendship of the group and we have admired the way the Society first managed to get established from very humble origins, has provided invaluable facilities and has grown and developed further in recent times.

I used to (and still do) put in recipes and other articles into the Wirral Society's monthly magazine. A little booklet called "Eat up your Greens" resulted and then the British Macular Disease Society picked up the idea for a larger recipe book. For my sins, I have been writing (and eating) my recipes and those of others ever since. It has been great fun.

The second charity is the **Foundation for Prevention of Blindness** and it brought me to Merseyside! Initially the charity was formed during the traumatic times before the St Paul's Eye Department in Old Hall Street closed its doors for the last time and moved in to become part of the Royal University Hospital. Essentially, it's initial role was to fund the first professorial chair for Ophthalmology in Merseyside so technically it was my boss! A good boss it turned out to be as it has supported research in St Paul's and the University of Liverpool right up to the present day. The Charity supports research, is creating laboratory space but it has a policy of "people first". In good times it has helped bring key research workers to Liverpool and when times have not been so good it has helped keep them here until alternative salaries and funds can be found.

Finally there is **Bradbury Fields** which used to be called Liverpool Voluntary Society for the Blind. Bradbury Fields is the granddad (or grandmother) of the bunch because I am reliably informed that it was around way back in the 19th century! In those times the society had the very limited brief of going around to blind people's homes and reading to them. I have this image in my head, which unfortunately cannot be far from the truth, of prim and proper Victorian ladies doing the rounds with a stout Bible in one hand and smelling salts in the other!

Thankfully Bradbury Fields has changed since those early days and now provides a huge range of services for blind and partially sighted people including rehabilitation, mobility, as well as services for those who are deaf as well as blind, help for blind and partially sighted children and specialised services for minority groups. They do numerous projects with local councils and provide extensive visual equality training. Most importantly they, as is the case with the other two charities, provide a friendly contact to those who need information and help. I'm sure you will agree with me when I say "Long may they all prosper!"

**Ian Grierson**

# WSBPS -
# Wirral Society of the Blind and Partially Sighted

*Sue Hadley with guide dog Amber, Lynne Sedgwick (Development Officer) and friend in the 'sensory garden'.*

The Wirral Society of the Blind and Partially Sighted was established in October 1989 by a group of visually impaired people. They included Bill Dowling, the first Chairman, Vera Steer, Derek Beauchamp, Irene Booth and Betty Robinson among others. Their aim was to create an organisation to offer help, support and advice to those with serious sight problems in Wirral. A constitution was written and an application for registration was submitted to the Charity Commission on 24th October 1989 when the Society became a registered charity. The group met in a variety of places including a Voluntary Service building, Church Halls and even members front rooms. It was decided that permanent premises would be needed to offer a full range of services and support for blind and partially sighted people. The search began! This was not going to be an easy task.

The Local Authority was approached and eventually after numerous meetings and correspondence, a disused, single story building on the corner of Birkenhead Park was offered on short term lease. In 1991, Ashville Lodge became the home of The Wirral Society of The Blind and Partially Sighted. The Building had been many things and had been used to store old furniture for two years before the Society came along. It had a hole in the roof and was in a poor state of repair. Many hands made light work, and in time Ashville Lodge was repaired, re-decorated and fitted out as a Resource Centre. A Development Officer was recruited who brought in volunteers to staff the centre and visit people in the community.

The Society has come a long way since 1989. The Centre was refurbished and extended in 1999 to accommodate the increase in service use over the years. Ashville Lodge was re-opened in year 2000 by the Duchess of Gloucester who was impressed by the work and achievements of The Society. Over the years we have established links with the RNIB and other local and National organisations and can offer a wide referral service for clients. We have built a positive working relationship with the NHS which has led us to providing an outreach information centre based at Arrowe Park Hospital. Our plans for the future will involve another building development project which will provide a purpose built facility for learning and Training. We are the only organisation based in Wirral offering support to this client group. We aim to provide the best and widest range of services for blind and partially sighted people with the mission statement of promoting well-being and independent living.

*Print enlarger to help with reading.*

An Eye For Good Food

We have met some remarkable people over the years, people who have influenced the Society and had a great deal to do with the growth and development making us what we are today. Donald Evans was an influential Chairperson of the Society who contributed to the society right up to his death in 2007. Donald had macular degeneration and lost the majority of his useful vision, this however, didn't hold him back in any way. Donald was a trained chef and spent most of his life in the hotel business and he certainly knew what went with good food, a good glass of wine! He was ever the optimist, his glass was always half full and never half empty. So, when you sample these scrumptious recipes, raise a glass to Donald, a lover of fine food and wine, and also partial to a good pint or two. Donald was supported over the years by Ray Hill who served as Vice Chairman from 1998 until April 2008 when Ray sadly died. Ray gave much of his valuable time, his wisdom and his commitment to supporting the Society and helping us move forward. He was a character who could sell ice to Eskimos, and he often did by helping to raise that extra bit of cash for the Society. If I were to compare Ray to a fine wine, it would have to be a sharp, crisp white with mellow undertones that could compliment any dish. He was an asset to the Society and is sadly missed.

*The meeting room for the WBPS*

Before I finish, I would like to mention one more person who I have the utmost respect for, our present Chairperson Susan Hadley. Sue has been involved with the Society for many years. Although Sue has always had sight problems, she lost all of her sight following an operation that unfortunately didn't have the positive results as hoped for. However, Sue has never let this hold her back in any way. In fact she has achieved so much over the past two years both with the development of the Society and her own personal challenges. Apart from completing the London Marathon in 2008, Sue has raised money for the Society through The Great North Run and a number of other challenging sponsored events. Sue lives her life to the full with high level walking and her love of the Lake District. She is a truly remarkable lady and an inspiration to those who are experiencing newly diagnosed eye conditions.

I would like to take this opportunity to thank our Patron and his wife, Ian and Dee Grierson for their support, time and creativity in writing this book. I hope you enjoy the recipes and thank you for your support.

**Lynne Sedgwick**
Development Officer
Wirral Society of The Blind and partially Sighted.

**WSBPS**
Wirral Society of the
Blind and Partially Sighted
Est. 1989

An Eye For Good Food

# The Foundation for Prevention of Blindness

The history of The Foundation starts with the move of St. Paul's Eye Hospital to new accommodation in the Royal Liverpool University Hospital in 1992. In fact St. Paul's is now in its third incarnation having originally started life in 1871 in No 6 St. Paul's Square in Liverpool 2. This was originally a prosperous part of Liverpool although by that time the area was starting a slow decline in fortunes. George Edward Walker, the original eye doctor, looked after patients in one room in the first hospital but after only a few years the work expanded to such an extent that a much larger building was needed.

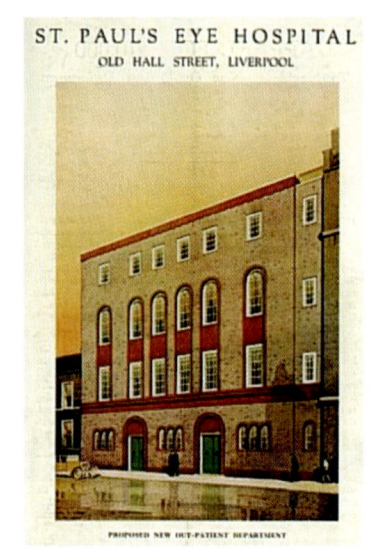

The new St. Paul's Eye Hospital opened its doors in 1912 on the corner of Old Hall Street and King Edward Street near the Northern General Hospital. It was opened by the 17th Lord Derby who had laid the foundation stone two years earlier. The hospital thrived throughout the 20th Century providing care to the people of Merseyside and beyond and introducing many ground breaking developments in eye care to the region. However by the late 1980s the style of health care had changed and the hospital had become somewhat isolated after the closure of the Northern. There was a need to expand surgery and outpatient specialisation and so a decision to move was made by the then Regional Health Authority.

Over the years the name "St. Paul's" had become embedded in the knowledge and affections of the people of Merseyside. Local businesses in the Old Hall Street area had also formed close links. So it was that the very generous donations of patients and well wishers together were combined with a grant from The Littlewoods Group to form the charity The Foundation for the Prevention of Blindness which was given the task of supporting the development of Academic Ophthalmology in Liverpool. Ian Grierson, the author of this book, was appointed and moved from London in 1992 to start a new Unit of Ophthalmology. In partnership with his clinical colleagues St.Paul's has now grown to a position of pre-eminence in the UK leading research into prevention and treatment of visual loss across a wide range of common and uncommon diseases. Numerous donors have supported The Foundation since its inception and the staff of St. Paul's have given their unstinting support, helping with many fundraising events from dinner dances to marathons!

The Foundation has raised nearly £4 million since 1992 which has been used to "pump prime" research initiatives including bring new specialists and academics to Liverpool, helping to train early researchers and providing start-up grants for equipment and laboratories. One of the major projects it has supported is the Clinical Eye Research Centre with was opened in 2006 by the 19th Earl Derby, whose grandfather had opened St. Paul's Eye Hospital in 1912. The Clinical Eye Research Centre shown on the left has given a new impetus to the search for treatments for eye disease by linking laboratory work with the specialist clinics elsewhere in the unit and will be the place where research ideas generated in the lab are first tested in patients in the future. Diseases being studied include glaucoma, diabetic retinopathy, macular degeneration, corneal disease and cancers of the eye. Several pioneering developments have been supported by the Foundation including the introduction of screening for diabetic retinopathy – one of the screening vans introduced in the late 1990s is shown on the right.

*A St Pauls ambulance for screening diabetic eye disease in the community.*

An Eye For Good Food

*St Paul's Square as it is now.*

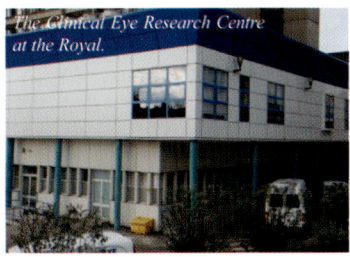

*The Clinical Eye Research Centre at the Royal.*

Thinking about the theme of this book reminds me of a couple of memories shared by past and present staff members. Cataract surgery has changed out of all recognition over the last 50 years. At its height St. Paul's Eye Hospital on Old Hall Street had over 100 beds with patients staying in hospital for very long periods of time. Stitches suitable for use in the eye had not yet been invented and so people who had had the surgery were kept on their backs in bed for three weeks at least with their heads held in place between sand bags and with a pad and bandage applied to the eye. Food was all pureed or mashed so that chewing was minimised. It was only in the late 1980s after cataract surgery had been completely transformed to the point of only one or two night stay that it came to light that the ban on pepper dating back to the 50s had been maintained. It was "policy" that patients should not have pepper on their food in case they sneezed and the eye was damaged. It was only through one gentleman complaining that his food was completely tasteless that the ban was eventually repealed!

The official history of St. Paul's records that in the early 1950s the Governors of the hospital were very concerned about the food intake of the nurses who lived there. So much so that to ensure the nurses were well cared for a package including fruit, vegetables and baked beans was delivered to the nurse rooms every Friday. This package made certain the nurses got their weekly allowance of vitamins. Looking through the recipes in this book I think that if we all follow at least some of them we won't need such direct support! The importance of good nutrition is becoming increasingly recognised in the prevention of eye disease as Ian writes later. On behalf of all of us working in the charity I would like to thank them both and wish them every success in continuing to promote healthy eating to the benefit of all our future health.

**Simon Harding**
Chairman
The Foundation for the Prevention of Blindness

**The Foundation for the Prevention of Blindness**
Registered Charity No: 1047988

# Bradbury Fields

**B**radbury Fields Services for Blind and Partially Sighted People, formerly Liverpool Voluntary Society for the Blind, was formed in 1857 by Mary Wainwright, who was determined to improve the lives of blind and partially sighted people in Liverpool. The charity has developed considerably over the 152 years of its existence and has grown beyond all recognition from the small society established in Victorian times. It has evolved in response to changing social trends and advances in technology. We now employ 32 staff, mostly on contract with local authorities, and are supported by more than 200 volunteers who help enable blind and partially sighted people to achieve their aspirations of living independent lives within the community.

*Jim Moran on the back of a bike for two.*

The Charity is situated at The Bradbury Centre and it is a purpose built centre for visually impaired people in the suburbs of Liverpool. It is the hub from which most of our services within the community are provided. We have close working relationships with many other organisations for visually impaired people and with other service providers within the statutory and voluntary sector.

We provide hospital advice services, assessment and rehabilitation training services to newly visually impaired (teaching them to regain independence through training in getting around, daily living skills, coping in their own homes, communication skills) and advice on disability benefits. Bradbury Fields also acts as a major provider of accessible information in Merseyside in Braille or alternatively on CD, cassette tape and large print on behalf of many suppliers of services from local councils, transport providers, health service providers as well as producing information on audio and electronic newsletters to more than 4,000 blind and partially sighted people throughout Liverpool and Knowsley.

Last year we supplied over 42,000 newsletters in audio format, providing information and important assistance for blind and partially sighted people helping them to stay independent within their own homes. We also provide a wide range of social opportunities, e.g., tandem clubs, art groups, music groups, daytime activities and walking groups, all these services being supported by our much valued, loyal volunteers and staff.

Our ethos is to enable blind and partially sighted people to achieve their personal goals and we are delighted that within this cook book all the recipes provided by ourselves were written and produced by Margaret Guppy, a former chef and member of our

*Communicating with the deaf and blind.*

Board of Trustees. Margaret herself is visually impaired. Bradbury Fields would like to thank you for purchasing this book. It is only by the support of the sighted community that we are able to provide such a wide range of services for blind and partially sighted adults and children of all ages.

An Eye For Good Food

Your support through donations, legacies or simply taking part in our fundraising helps us to deliver a service to blind and partially sighted people in Liverpool. We very much hope you enjoy the recipes without worrying about your waistline!

**James A Moran**
Chief Executive
Bradbury Fields

*Bradbury Fields is also about having fun!*

# Homage to Home Cooking
# (We are what we Eat – Unfortunately!)

It is believed in many quarters that good diet can protect us from the ravages of some of the well known eye diseases such as Age Related Macular Degeneration (AMD), cataract and diabetic eye disease. Insufficient food intake and poor quality diet are equally bad for us because in such circumstances we lack the essential nutrients that protect the body from all kinds of assault. One form of internal attack that is dangerous, particularly to the retina (AMD) and lens (cataract), is oxidative damage. Delicate eye tissues can be destroyed by the ravages of highly reactive molecules that are produced as a bi-product of the normal day-to-day activities. The main activity of the eye is focusing and then converting light into electrical impulses. About 70% of all the sensory nerves in the body are located in the eye and virtually all of them reside in the retina. The impulses are then transported by the optic nerve to the brain where they become "sight" as we know it.

Around 70% of all the sensory neurones of the body live in the eye and all these ocular cells and nerves need protection because for the most part they have to last us a lifetime. Unfortunately nerves do not replace themselves as can occur for many cells elsewhere in the body. For the necessary protection we rely on a range of substances including antioxidant vitamins (vitamins C, E and beta carotene), minerals (zinc and selenium), fatty acids (omega-3), detoxifying enzymes (super oxide dismutase, catalase) and, particularly important for the macula and lens, carotenoids (lutein, zeaxanthin). Collectively they mount the defence that we need to keep our eyes healthy and, for that matter, they contribute in no small way to the well being of our whole body. For the most part we gain these substances from the food we eat as micronutrients.

Some people despite what they do will end up with macular degeneration, cataract or one of the other eye conditions. On the other hand, many people could delay the onset, decrease the severity or even prevent their problem altogether if they had a better diet. Essentially we need to be much more aware of how and where our food is being produced, how it is being processed and prepared and what exactly it is that is going into our mouths when we eat. I do think we are becoming deskilled both in terms of our basic knowledge of food and how to prepare it so it is both tasty and nutritious. One of my favourite food writers is Michael Pollon and a quote from him might be "Eat food not industrialised food-like products" and perhaps our recipe book may help towards that difficult goal?

As you may gather, the recipes in this book are wholesome rather than overly healthy – there is not a lot of balsamic vinegar or couscous around but plenty of butter, eggs and sugar! I've had a number of people say – "after Vegetables for Vision and Fruit for Vision (two recipe books published and sold by the Macular Disease Society), isn't this book a bit away from your usual message?". In one sense they are right – the book is not dominated by a load of fruit and vegetable recipes and the calorie count is a bit on the high side in some of the recipes. However the book is very much centred on home cooking and there is nothing wrong with good old fashioned home cooking as far as I am concerned. Let us all do a little bit more home cooking and we as a nation will be a lot healthier and I think a lot happier.

We have been practising home cooking for over a million years; ever since our remote ancestors discovered fire. Obviously cooking made some tough plants, seeds and vegetable products edible (early bread). Dubious old carcasses found on the plains were important food and energy sources for ancient man but if the meat had gone off badly they could be killers – cooking meat destroyed a lot of the germs and, within strict limits, made this scavenging activity much safer. Home cooking increased the overall population and had some increased survival value. From then until now we have had the best part of a million years of progressive home cooking development although in the last 50 years a proportion of us have gone back to the ways of the earliest hunter gather peoples. They have dispensed with all the hard earned culinary skills acquired by our fore bearers and regressed to being grazers, albeit that all the grazing in modern times is done from the fridge rather than on the plains of the Serengetti.

Since its very modest beginnings cooking has become more and more sophisticated and diverse so that when we come up to more modern times food and cooking are a matter of national pride (the cuisines of France, India and Italy for example). In fact the populations of most countries revere eating and they have considerable enthusiasm for their national dishes and way of cooking. These enthusiasms border on the ridiculous in some countries where their cuisine is seen as essential to their self perceived idea of national identity and civilisation. However it must be said that the institution of home cooking with family meals around the dining table is seen World Wide as the only way to eat – cooking and knowledge of good food are essential whether you are rich or poor, female or male.

Unfortunately there are exceptions to the rule and some quite extreme exceptions at that. One of the countries where the belief in the importance of good food and the social value of collective home cooked family meals is definitely on the wane is England. You might say that that cannot be true after all we live in a society that is fixated with celebrity chefs, cooking books dominate the non-fiction shelves of our book shops (may I say at this point a very personal "thank goodness"), British restaurants are prominent in the lists of the best in the World and you cannot turn on the TV without finding a cooking programme of some sort. All of these are facts but they are misleading facts, more to do with how we would like to think of ourselves than actuality and do not really represent Britain as it is today.

The reality is that for too many British families, home cooking is a thing of the past. Sales of dining tables are at an all time low (and were so before recession set in), ovens in many kitchens are hardly used and a high percentage of people profess to have no cooking skills at all. We seem to get by these days by grazing, when we need to, on cold food from the fridge. Hot food is too often a take away delivered to the door or a ready meal stuck in the microwave for a few minutes. Of course we know this so no one should be surprised that we are top of the European league for the consumption of factory processed foods, crisps and ready meals stuffed with preservatives and E numbers. What is shocking is the extent of our corruption to the "dark side" of bad eating habits. It appears to be the case that our 50-60 million "Brits" eat more crisps and ready meals than the rest of Europe (500 million) put together! We seem to be totally besotted by convenience foods that are made of poor quality produce and so full of additives they make our children hyperactive and do our long term health no good at all.

No one wants to be ripped off but we as a Nation are obsessed with the cost of food. Too often we worry about the expense of a chicken and not enough over the quality of the meat. The dictum that "cheap and nutritious is good but cheap and unhealthy is not so good" should be self evident but often it is not. We have poor regard for where our food comes from and what precisely it is made up of! These all combine to put us at short term risk of food poisoning (food poisoning outbreaks are ridiculously high in the UK) and long term risk of being poorly equipped to hold chronic illness at bay (too many additives and too few nutrients in our food). Our European neighbours regard our eating habits with emotions ranging from amusement to horror - an Italian chef once said of the British "they would rather buy a good suit than good food, yet a suit can be thrown away whereas food becomes part of you!". Here is the crux of the issue, we just don't seem to think of food as any more than fuel to be taken in with as much speed and as little ceremony as possible. Home cooking almost always involves better food than you get from a convenience pack, it gives you an excuse to use the dinner table and reduces stress by taking time out of our busy lives to relax.

The Daily Mirror newspaper had an article by Jacqui Morrell in 2008 that stated "80% of the Nation is eating too much saturated fat" and some regions are far poorer than others. The worst of all is our region the North West of England where the fat intake is the highest in England with a whopping great intake of 44 grams of fat per day compared to London and the South East with a still high but more respectable 24 grams of fat per day. Our book cannot claim to be packed with health conscious recipes but none the less I recommend it - we all need to do a bit more home cooking and eat a little less factory produced gloop than most of us seem to be doing at present. Am I a paragon of virtue? Certainly not! To give you an example, last Saturday my main meal of the day was a ready meal (full of fat and salt and totally unwholesome) while watching football on the TV. To make things even worse my dining table was one of my "health conscious" recipe books serving as an impromptu tray! Now how bad is that!

**Ian Grierson**

An Eye For Good Food

# SOUPS & STARTERS

There is quite a varied mixture of different types of dish in this section from the simple to the more exotic.

# HAM & PEA SOUP

(Aimee Livingstone from Wavertree for the Foundation)

*My Mother-in-Law, Maureen, always says a good soup "has to have eating and drinking in it". Aimee's Pea and Ham soup certainly passes the Mother in Law test with flying colours!*

(Serves 6)

## STOCK

1 small onion cut in half
1 large carrot cut in half
1 celery stick cut in half
1 leek (white only cut in half)
1 garlic clove crushed
1 bay leaf
6 sprigs of thyme
4 black peppercorns
1 ham hock with 2L (about 3 ½ pts) of water

## SOUP

50g (under 2oz) butter
200g (around 7oz) of sliced shallots
75g (2 ½ oz) of chopped pancetta
1 garlic clove crushed
680g (1 ½ lbs) of frozen peas (defrosted)
2 smoked rashers of bacon cut in 1cm lengths

**Combine all the stock ingredients into a large (very large) heavy-based pan (pressure cooker pan would do without the lid). Boil everything for about 2 hours at medium heat skimming the surface of the stock when needed. Remove, cool and sieve the liquid, reserving the ham to one side. Start the soup by heating the butter in a large pan then adding the shallots, pancetta and garlic sweating on low heat for up to 15 minutes until the shallots are tender. Add in the stock and bring to the boil and skim if required. Introduce 500g of peas for a few minutes then puree in a liquidiser or using a hand blender – add a little extra water if the soup is too thick for you. Just before serving the soup you need to cook the remaining peas, fry the bacon until crisp, flake any ham from the hock you wish to use. Divide the peas and ham between 6 bowls, pour on the soup, scatter on the bacon and enjoy with crusty bread.**

An Eye For Good Food

# GOAT'S CHEESE & COURGETTE SOUP

(Dr Luminita Paraoan, from Liverpool for the Foundation)

*Dr Paraoan runs a research team based in the University of Liverpool and is part of St Pauls Eye Unit that conducts fundamental laboratory investigations into key eye problems like Age Related Eye Disease. Some of her key funding has come from the Foundation.*

**(Approximate quantities for 4 people)**

150g (about 4 ½ oz) of goat cheese (any type – hard, soft etc)
5 medium sized courgettes sliced into rings
3 cloves of garlic chopped fine
800ml (1 ½ pts) of milk
15ml (1tblsp) olive oil
15ml (1tblsp) each of fresh dill, basil and parsley chopped
(Salt and pepper)

**Fry the garlic on low heat in the olive oil for 1 min, add the courgettes and stir them in until softened, puree using a hand blender, a processor or a sieve and finally add the cheese. Put the mixture together with warm milk in a pan on gentle heat allowing the cheese to melt and mix through the soup. If you want to thin the soup a little add in up to 250ml of hot water, season to taste and serve with the chopped fresh herbs scattered in right at the end.**

An Eye For Good Food

# MUSHROOM SOUP

(Keith Ryan from Wirral for the WSBPS)

*Keith is a volunteer at Ashville lodge (WSBPS) and this is one of his own creations – well done Keith, it is a delicious combination of mushroom and cheese. Keith says the soup is nice warm or cold and if you don't like Stilton then the soup is fine without it.*

(A nice starter for 4 but a whole meal for 2)

350g (12oz) sliced mushrooms
1 medium red onion, finely chopped
550ml (1pt) of chicken (or vegetable) stock
100g (over 3oz) of Stilton cheese
30ml (2tblsps) of butter

**Melt the butter in a pan then add the onions and mushrooms and cook until soft. Then add in the chicken stock and stir contents repeatedly and introduce the cheese a little at a time. Keith says it is important to stir and taste and when right for you blitz with a hand blender to get a nice thick consistency. Serve hot or cold with crusty bread.**

# ASPARAGUS & MINT SOUP

(Dr Helen Orton, for the Foundation)

*Helen's day job is head of teaching for Orthoptics and Vision Sciences in Liverpool University. Also she is a really fine cook and caterer so I am delighted that she has given us some of her recipes. Asparagus is a fabulous tasting and nutritious vegetable – packed with goodness.*

(Masses for 6 and plenty for 8)

30g (1oz) of butter
10ml (2tsps) of olive oil
2 medium potatoes – peeled and chopped into 2cm cubes
3 small leeks- trimmed and sliced into 2cm pieces
500g (1lb 2oz) asparagus tips – cut into 2cm lengths (reserve a few tips for decoration)
15ml (1tblsp) of chopped mint
2.4L (4pts) of chicken stock
30ml (2tblsps) of single cream

**Chop the asparagus leaving the tips aside. Melt the butter in a large pan and then add in the chopped leeks, potatoes and stir for 5 minutes. Add in the stock and bring to a simmer then after 5 minutes add in the asparagus stalks and cook for a further 7 minutes without a lid on the pan. Meanwhile add olive oil to a frying pan, warm and add the asparagus tips. Blend the mixture and season. Add cream and decorate with the cooked asparagus tips.**

An Eye For Good Food

# REALLY RED SOUP

(Ian Grierson)

*I complained to a friend of mine that my tomato soup lacked colour and he said that in his homeland in Eastern Europe it was common to make soup out of tomatoes and peppers and that the red peppers gave good colour. My first version did not have the mountains of paprika he uses and was a little bland so I added orange (being recently back from Florida where they put oranges into everything). I was proud of my invention until one day I picked up a recipe magazine and there it was – a soup of oranges, tomatoes and red peppers just like my own. There is nothing new is there? However such a mixture is both nutritious and delicious so it is not at all surprising that someone was there long before me.*

**(Enough for 4)**

6 tomatoes
1L (1.8pts) of passata (good tomato juice)
450g (1lb) jar of red peppers (roasted type)
500 ml (slightly less than 1pt) chicken stock
250 ml (10floz) of orange juice
2.5ml (½ tsp) paprika
2.5ml (½ tsp) pepper
5ml (1tsp) sugar

**Chop the tomatoes roughly and the drained peppers and add them to a blender along with half of the passata plus the paprika and sugar. Blend well together. Thereafter pass though a colander into a pan and add in the remaining ingredients. Heat up and simmer for 10 to 15 minutes. Serve with rolls.**

An Eye For Good Food

# EASY VEGETABLE SOUP

(Ian Grierson)

*This soup came out of the times when "two for the price of one" bargains were all the rage in supermarkets. Being Scots I could not resist these offers even if I did not need the extra food. So we used to get two bags of pre-chopped vegetables; one we needed for dinner and the other got made into this soup with any extra left over vegetables that happen to be around.*

(Plenty for 4 and even enough for 6)

1 or 2 bags (around 700g to 800g) of supermarket mixed chopped vegetables
1 onion
1 large potato
1 ½ - 2L (3 to 3 ½ pts) of water
2 chicken stock cubes
5ml (1tsp) of curry powder
5ml (1tsp) dried coriander

**Chop up the onion and fry it off in a reasonable sized pan for 1 minute or so and then add in the sliced potato, curry and coriander powder. Coat them and then add in warm water, stock cubes and the bag of vegetables. Bring to the boil and reduce heat to a gentle simmer cooking the soup with the lid on for about 40 minutes. After that time add lots of pepper and some salt to taste then blitz with a hand blender and serve.**

## FAST PEA SOUP

(Ian Grierson)

*It is the case that there is often as much if not more vitamin C in frozen than fresh peas, certainly if your fresh peas have travelled far or are near their sell by date they will have lost a lot of this delicate water soluble vitamin. This is a simple and fast soup that we make all year round.*

(Plenty for 4)

2 garlic cloves
15ml (1tblsp) of olive oil
900g (2lbs) of frozen peas defrosted
1.2L (2pts) chicken stock (any you like)
15ml (1tblsp) fresh mint or 5ml (1tsp) dried mint
(Salt and pepper)

**Chop up the garlic and fry gently in the oil at the base of a reasonable sized pan for 1 to 2 minutes. Add in the peas and mint (if dried) and coat with oil, then introduce the stock giving a good stir. Bring to the boil and simmer for 15 minutes then let the soup cool a little before blitzing in a food processor or with a hand blender. Then season with a little salt and a lot of pepper.**

## LETTUCE SOUP

(Margaret Guppy from Liverpool for Bradbury Fields)

*Margaret has a long association with Bradbury Fields and has been building up a recipe collection with the intention of writing her own cookery book and has donated many of them to this project. Excellent they are too, so good that all Bradbury Field's submissions are from Margaret.*

(Servings for 4)

1 medium potato peeled and diced
1.2L (2pts) chicken stock
15ml (1tblsp) vegetable oil
1 loose leaf lettuce coarsely chopped
(Salt and pepper to taste)
30ml (2tblsps) of single cream
Chopped chives for decoration

**Place the vegetable oil in a saucepan and add the diced potato, stirring gently, cook for 3 mins. Add in the vegetable stock and any seasoning to the pan and cook at medium heat for 20 mins. Half way through the cooking time add in th chopped lettuce. At the end of cooking liquidize the contents of the pan until smooth, return to the heat and when just off the boil serve up with a drizzle of cream and some chopped chives.**

An Eye For Good Food

# SPINACH & WATERCRESS SOUP

(Marie and Paul Hiscott from Hoylake for the Foundation)

*Paul is a Pathology Professor who has a special interest in eyes and he and I have worked together for many years. I have never thought of Paul as much of a cook but Marie is great. One of them has to be because they have rather a large family.*

(For up to 8)

1 large leek
1 large potato (peeled and chopped into small pieces)
200g (between 6 and 7 oz) bag of spinach
50g (under 2oz) of watercress
30g (1oz) of rocket
Olive oil
Knob of butter
1.2L (around 2 pts) of vegetable stock
1.25ml (¼ tsp) grated nutmeg
(Salt and pepper)

**Was and chop the leeks and sweat them off in oil and butter for 10 mins. Add potato and continue sweating for a further 5 mins. Add the stock and simmer for 10 mins then add the spinach and watercress to the soup, keep cooking for 2 more mins until spinach has wilted then remove from the heat. Finally add in the rocket and liquidize (hand blender will do). Add nutmeg and season to taste, Reheat if you need to and serve with crusty bread.**

An Eye For Good Food

# BORSCHT

(Teri Holmes from Wirral for the WSBPS)

*I was in the restaurant of an old museum in what was then called East Berlin, it was my first time on the "wrong side" of the Berlin Wall and I was waiting for soup and sandwiches. I was not at ease, to my mind everyone around me looked like secret police even the old lady in the corner doing needle work! In came this purple liquid in a cracked tin plate – were they out to poison me? Not at all, it was Borscht and it was delicious. Thanks for this one Terri do try it but not in a cracked tin plate.*

(Should be enough for 6)

3 fresh beetroot finely grated
1 onion sliced thinly
¼ of a red cabbage grated
About 800ml (1 ½ pts) of vegetable stock
15ml (1tblsp) of lemon juice
5ml (1tsp) brown sugar
15ml (1tblsp) fresh chopped parsley
15ml (1tblsp) fresh chopped chives
140ml (¼ pt) of plain yoghurt

**Put the vegetables and the stock into a pan which you bring to the boil and then simmer for 20 mins. Add in the lemon juice and sugar and season. Blend to make the soup smooth and serve up with a swirl of yogurt and a sprinkle of the chopped herbs.**

# THAI BREAKFAST SOUP (KAO TOM)

(Dr Robert Ritch from New York for the Foundation)

*Professor Ritch is a close friend of the Liverpool Eye Department for many years. He is the Professor of Clinical Ophthalmology and Director of Glaucoma Services at the World Famous New York Eye and Ear Infirmary. That is his day job but he is, in his other guise, an excellent cook with an enthusiasm for South East Asian cuisine. Bob has given us his version of a classic Thai morning soup that he says "sure beats bacon and eggs or bagels".*

**(Serves 2-4)**

150g (4oz) of any pre-cooked chopped up cold meat (if you wish), ham or well cooked bacon is fine, cooked chicken works well and prawns or crab sticks are in keeping (you will not need so much of these). Additional garnish would include 2 chopped spring onions, finely chopped fresh ginger to taste, 1 red or green chilli deseeded and chopped up fine and chopped fresh coriander.

100g (3oz) previously cooked long grain rice
1.2L (2pts) chicken stock
45ml (3tblsps) fish sauce
30ml (2tblsps) vegetable oil
3 clove of garlic well chopped
(plenty of black pepper)
15ml (1tblsp) vegetable oil
30ml (2 tblsps) finely chopped garlic (easy garlic if you wish)

**Heat oil in a decent sized pan and gently cook the garlic for 1 minute remove, reserve and wipe pan with kitchen towel. Combine the cooked rice and stock in this pan, bring up to the boil and keep at a simmer. Add the fish sauce and lots of pepper and maintain simmering for 5 minutes. Add garlic and the rest of the garnishes including the meat if you have some. Serve immediately.**

# TOMATO & SPAGHETTI STARTER

(Dave Evans from Morton, Wirral for the WSBPS)

*Dave runs a Health and Safety Business and does training for WSBPS he is also an excellent cook. This spaghetti and tomato dish is a simple and nutritious starter that can be a filling lunch. It is a real store cupboard "life saver" when you have nothing obvious to make and any past will do. Anchovies are really good for you and we don't eat them as often as we should.*

**(For 6 people as a starter or a lunch for 3 or 4)**

400g (14oz) of dried spaghetti
45ml (3tblsps) olive oil
1 jar of anchovy fillets
440g tin of chopped tomatoes
15ml (1tblsp) tomato puree
5ml (1tsp) chilli sauce
6 asparagus spears from a jar
6 stoned olives (green or black)
2 cloves of garlic sliced
15ml (1tblsp) capers
5ml (1tsp) Italian dried spices
(Pepper to season)

**Heat the olive oil in a frying pan and pour in all the anchovies and break them up while they are frying. When the fish are pulped, add in the garlic, stir around and add the tomatoes, puree, chopped olives, chopped asparagus, dried spice and chilli sauce. Cook for 15 mins by which time the sauce will be thicker and add plenty of pepper. Cook the spaghetti according to packet instructions in a large pan of slightly salted water. Drain and add the spaghetti to the sauce in a serving dish – 1st course done as simple as that!**

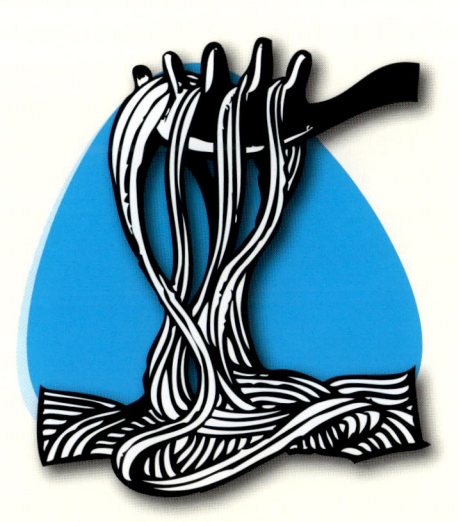

An Eye For Good Food

# FAIL SAFE RISSOTO

(Dr Fiona Rowe from Merseyside for the Foundation)

*Fiona is a senior lecturer in Orthoptics at the University of Liverpool who is a national representative on several important committees for blindness and visual impairment. It takes a cleaver individual to produce an "easy risotto" recipe that works and this she has managed to do. She says "you can add sautéd mushrooms, crabmeat, prawns, asparagus etc – or just enjoy it plain". I like her idea of the plain risotto with maybe peas as a starter or lunch but put it with pan fried sea bass on the side and here is a very special dinner full of nutritious goodness and plenty of different textures and tastes.*

(Starter for 4 people)

30ml (2 tblsps) of olive oil
1 medium onion finely diced
3 garlic cloves
1 mug (200g or so) of Arborio rice
200g (7oz) of frozen or fresh garden peas
150ml (6 floz) of white wine
1L (1 ¾ pts) of chicken stock
60g (2oz) of butter
125g (4oz) of Parmaggiano cheese (any hard Italian cheese)

**Gently fry the onion and crushed garlic in olive oil for 2 mins and then add in all the rice making sure that all the rice is coated with oil and the onion well mixed in and then add the wine stirring well. Start adding in the chicken stock a little at a time allowing it to absorb. By around 15 mins add in the peas, mix well and add more stock continuing for another 15 mins by which time the rice will have softened. Add grated cheese and knobs of butter, stir them in, take off the heat, put on a lid and leave for a further 5 mins. Stir for a last time and serve.**

# STUFFED SWEET PEPPERS

(Mrs Silva Grosu from Bucharest, Rumania for the Foundation)

*Turkey mince is much lower in fat than the usual lamb or beef mince so it is healthier. Although a little lack of body means, in my opinion, it does not quite make as nice standard meals. Here, however, is a recipe from Silva, that brings out the best in turkey mince.*

(Starter for 12 or a lunch for 6)

12 medium sized peppers of any colour (try a mix of colours)
750g (slightly under 1 ½ lb) turkey mince (pork mince will do)
1 slice of thick white bread soaked in water
1 onion finely chopped
45ml (3tblsps) of rice
Handful of fresh dill chopped finely (tsp of dried dill)

### SEASONING
Handful of fresh parsley chopped (tsp of dried parsley)
30ml (2tblsps) vegetable oil
30ml (2tblsps) tomato puree or paste
15ml (1tblsp) white flour
225g (½ pt) water
Tub of crème fraîche or sour cream

**For the stuffing, fry the onion and rice in oil for 3 minutes then add water (watch out for splashing) and cook further when you have added in the mince, bread and herbs. Season before serving.**

**Prepare the peppers by cutting around the stem and taking out the seeds. Fill them with the rice and mince mixture and put them standing in an oven dish with lid. Cook the tomatoes in oil adding the flour and a bit of water and pour the sauce on the peppers. Put a lid on the peppers and cook for 40 mins in a preheated oven (1900C) and serve.**

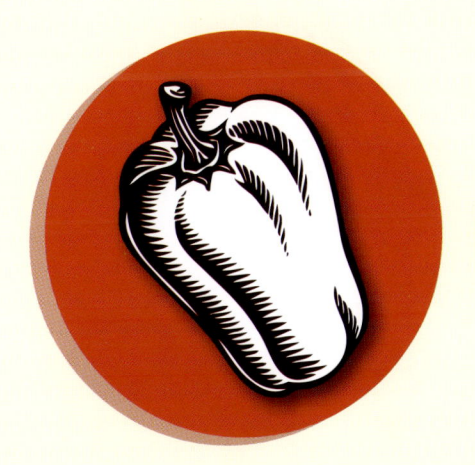

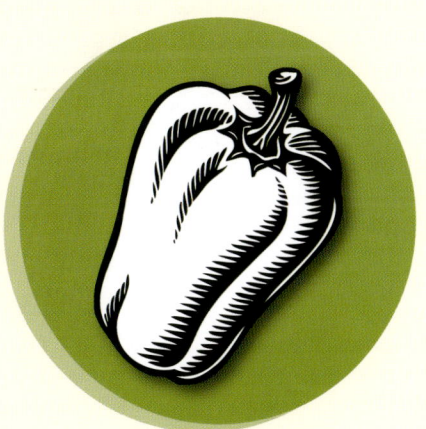

An Eye For Good Food

# RAMSWORTH AVOCADOS

(Trevor Holland from Windemere Manor Hotel for the WSBPS)

*I read somewhere that 75% of people in the UK have never eaten an avocado. It seems an awfully lot of people who haven't even tried one of nature's important fruits that provide plenty of the good unsaturated fats, antioxidant vitamin E and lots of vitamin C.*

n/a

2 large ripe avocados
15ml (1tblsp) lemon juice
100g (3oz) canned, frozen or fresh crab meat
100g (3oz) shrimps or prawns
60ml (4tblsps) mayonnaise
60ml (4tblsps) chopped chives
10ml (2tsps) red wine vinegar
1 egg white

**Halve the avocados, remove stones and brush with lemon juice to prevent browning. Mix crab, cooked prawns (chopped), mayonnaise, chives and red wine vinegar. Wisk egg white until it stands in stiff peaks. Fold carefully into the crab mixture and pile the crab mix into halved avocados. Place in a shallow dish and pour round a little water and bake in an oven at 180°C for 20-25 minutes when they should be golden brown.**

An Eye For Good Food

# SCOTTISH PATTIES FOR BREAKFAST

(Sue Hadley from Wirral for the WSBPS)

*Sue is the current chairperson for the Wirral Society for the Blind and Partly Sighted. These patties Sue says are "a good alternative to sausages with a cooked breakfast". I also think they make a nice starter with a few salad leaves and some chutney.*

**(6 people for starter)**

500g (1lb 2oz) of pork mince
500g (1lb 2oz) of beef mince
2.5ml (½ tsp) of salt
5ml (1tsp) of ground white pepper
60g (2oz) of breadcrumbs
5ml (1tsp) of ground coriander
2.5g (½ tsp) ground ginger
1 beaten egg

**Add the mince, seasoning, spices and breadcrumbs together and mix well in a mixing bowl and bind in the beaten egg. It may be helpful to add a little water but not very much when you are making patties out of the mixture. You can cook the patties in the oven at 180°C for around 20 minutes or alternatively fry in oil in a frying pan.**

# HAM PARCELS

(Dee Grierson)

*Dee believes in keeping everything as simple as possible and this is a quick starter that she can delegate even to me with a reasonable expectation of a result.*

**(For 4 people)**

12 slices of Parma ham
225g (½ lb) of cream cheese
6 large or 12 small dried figs

**Take the figs and if they are large cut them in half, smother the figs with cream cheese, wrap them up with a slice of ham to each and pin them with a cocktail stick if needed. Three per portion on a few salad leaves would make a reasonable starter. Mascarpone or cottage cheese could be used instead of standard cream cheese if preferred.**

# SAN DIEGO STARTER

(Ian Grierson)

*It may be a long way to Tipperary but it is even longer to San Diego, California especially if you go via Chicago as I did recently. I was thoroughly tired when I arrived at my hotel and more than a little despondent because I knew that I had the return trip tomorrow night to look forward to. However that was tomorrow night not today, I met a couple of friends, and I realised I was starving. We had a glorious steak dinner in the hotel but I just loved the tastes in their simple starter. This is my version of it.*

**(For 4)**

2 Romaine lettuce
2 pears
2 red apples
45ml (3tblsps) of orange juice
30ml (2tblsps) of caster sugar
125g (4oz) packet or tin of crushed walnuts
125ml (5 floz) of blue cheese dressing

**Cut the apples and pears into segments; core them but don't skin them unless the skin is thick. Cook them in the orange juice and sugar for around 5 mins or so. Make a fan with a few lettuce leaves, put a scoop of apple/pear mixture at the base, scatter on some walnut, drizzle over some of the dressing and serve.**

# GARLIC MUSHROOMS

(Margaret Guppy from Liverpool for Bradbury Fields)

*Garlic mushrooms are such a favourite in our family; both are central to the French style of cooking but actually were established first in Italian cookery and then brought to France by Catherine de Medici in the 16th century. Thanks Catherine and also thanks to Margaret for the recipe.*

**(Serves 4)**

350g (12oz) small button mushrooms
45g (1 ½ oz) of butter
1 fat clove of garlic
Salt and pepper to taste
150ml ( ¼ pt or so) of double cream

**Wash the mushrooms and trim off the stalk ends. Melt the butter in a pan and add the mushrooms and chopped garlic and cook for 5 mins. Season and slowly stir in the cream cooking gently for a further 5 mins. Serve hot in ramekins or small dishes.**

An Eye For Good Food

# MUSHROOMS IN PORT

(Margaret Guppy from Liverpool for Bradbury Fields)

*This is another excellent and tasty mushroom dish from Margaret and she says Madeira or cream sherry can be used instead of port.*

**(Serves 4 as a supper and 6 as a starter)**

100g (little more than 3oz) of butter
1onion peeled and finely chopped
450g (1lb) of mushrooms with stalks removed
60ml (4tblsps) ruby port
Salt and pepper
30ml (2tblsps) of double cream
4-6 slices of bread with the crusts removed

**Melt half the butter in a frying pan and add the chopped onions and cook until they are soft. Then bring in the mushrooms and fry them gently for 3 to 5 mins. Stir in the port at this stage and cook it out for a further 3 mins. Add the cream and cook gently for only a min then remove the pan from the heat. Fry the bread in the remaining butter and serve as a base topped with the mushrooms and sauce.**

# WELSH RAREBIT

(Margaret Shields from Dovecot, Liverpool for the Foundation)

*Margret says "a real Welsh version of rarebit that is made with sharp Cheddar cheese and fresh thyme". A classic!*

**(A starter for 4 or a lunch for 2)**

225g (8oz) grated sharp (mature) cheddar or another hard cheese
55ml (3 ½ tblsps) of good ale
30ml (2tblsps) English mustard
15ml (1 tblsp) chopped fresh thyme
4 slices of bread
(seasoning)

**Combine the cheese, ale, mustard, thyme and seasoning in a small pan over low heat and gently melt stirring occasionally until smooth. Grill one side of bread in grill pan then turn over, pour on mixture and grill further for about 1 min and eat immediately. If you want Margaret says just to make toast and pour on the hot mixture and eat without grilling.**

SOUPS & STARTERS

An Eye For Good Food

# SARDINE PATÉ

(Margaret Guppy from Liverpool for Bradbury Fields)

*A tin of sardines and a tub of cream cheese are such good things to have as standby; here is an excellent starter or just a glorious late supper.*

(Enough for 4)

225g (8oz) tin of sardines
110g (4oz) of butter
110g (4oz) of cream cheese
Juice of ½ a lemon
2.5ml (½ tsp) French mustard
(Seasoning)

**Beat the sardines with half the oil in the tin into the mixture of butter and cream cheese (Margaret says it can be all butter if you prefer) until well blended together. Then introduce the lemon juice, mustard and seasoning. Serve up either in individual ramekins or on a small plate dish. Decorate with dill or chives and eat with fingers of hot toast.**

# BEANS & PASTA

(Keith Teare from Oxton, Wirral for WSBPS)

*Good starter that with strong pesto flavours so a little goes a long way in this dish.*

(Plenty for 4 and can stretch to 6)

210g (7oz) young broad beans
210g (7oz) of green beans
30ml (2tblsps) of virgin olive oil
15ml (1tblsp) of shop bought pesto
300g (10oz) of dried pasta (Penne or Tagliatelle work well)
45g (3tblsps) of grated Parmesan cheese
Black pepper for seasoning

**Cook the beans together in boiling salted water for no more than 15 mins. Drain them and add pesto and oil and mix well in the pan add extra pesto if you wish. At the same time cook the pasta according to packet instructions (usually between 10 and 15 mins). Drain the pasta and add it to the beans and mix well. Plate out and scatter grated cheese on each.**

An Eye For Good Food

# MACKEREL PATÉ

(Ian Grierson)

*Our neighbour Jim has just delivered some fresh mackerel so all the talk is about cutting heads off (more likely to be ours than the fishes), gutting and the lack of a good filleting knife. We are determined to have mackerel so I will get some of the smoked variety from the local store and make a pate just as a stand by (all this head chopping and gutting has quite put me off the real thing). As it turned out the fresh mackerel was simply delicious but so was the paté.*

(For 6)

Packet (around 450g or 1lb) of smoked mackerel (can get away with less)
2 cloves of garlic
5ml (1tsp) of paprika
2 lemons
275ml (½ pt) of plain yoghurt
12 slices of bread

**Take the flesh off the smoked mackerel and get rid of the skin and bones. Put the fish in a food processor along with the yoghurt, the juice of one lemon and paprika and blitz until reasonably smooth. Keep in the fridge for about 1 hour and serve up with toast and slices of lemon.**

# SALMON LOAF

(Margaret Guppy from Liverpool for Bradbury Fields)

*Margaret says that her recipe came originally from the Amish Community of the USA and is a perfect starter with Melba toast and can be a main meal with salad.*

(8 people can get a taste in a starter but the loaf is a nice main meal for 4)

450g (1lb) of salmon
100g (4oz) of softened butter
2.5ml (½ tsp) salt and pepper to taste
275ml (½ pt) of warm milk
4 eggs well beaten

**Heat the oven to 180°C and grease a medium sized loaf tin. Break up the salmon and mix all the ingredients together. Then place the loaf tin in a roasting tin that is ½ filled with water and cook for 1 hr.**

An Eye For Good Food

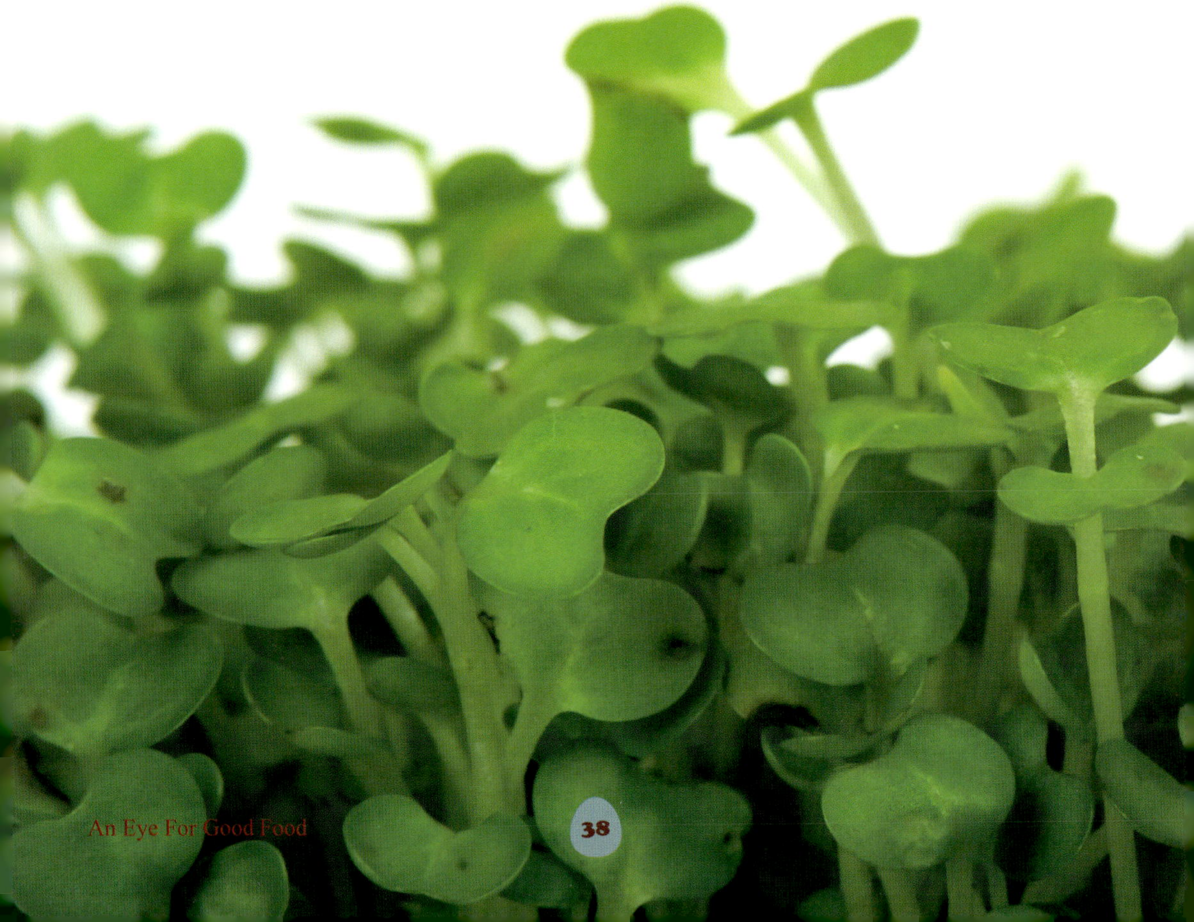

# Salads

The salads from me (IG) were the ones we had at our "Soup and Salad" day for the WBPS in June 2009. We thought it would be nice to publish all the recipes in this book. Along with those are some excellent contributions from others that we may pirate them for another "Soup and Salad" day in the future.

# LARGE TIN OF SALMON (salad)

(Ian Grierson)

*This is a simple salad I created (which means I probably read it somewhere) to eke out a tin of salmon and try and make a bit of a meal out of it. The dish works as a lunch-time salad or as easy to prepare starter with biscuits.*

**(Enough with bread for a lunch for 2 or 3 people or with crackers a starter for 4 or more)**

Large (400g) tin of salmon
Small tin (200g) of sweet corn
½ red pepper
2 spring onions
6-8 capers
3 small pickled gherkins (cornichones)
5ml (1tsp) paprika
30ml (2 tblsps) mayonnaise
½ a cucumber
Packet (100g) of rocket leaves

**Drain the salmon but not completely and put in a mixing bowl with the fully drained tin of sweet corn. Chop up the pepper, spring onions, gherkins and capers. Mix paprika, chopped salad, salmon and mayonnaise all together to a consistency you like. Scatter rocket on a plate and mound the salmon in the middle. Slice the cucumber long ways into straps and drape them round the salmon.**

# ORANGE & OLIVE SALAD

(Ian Grierson)

*I usually refer to this as the 2 Os salad and when I stayed for a while in Egypt this was one of my favourites. It is tasty, full of vitamins and carries a little bit of sunshine with it even on a cold day in Britain. The use of cinnamon (I have cut back on it) might seem a strange choice for a salad for our palate but cinnamon is widely used in "savoury" dishes in many parts of North Africa and the Middle East.*

**(A nice taster for 4)**

3 Clementines (or Satsuma's or whatever available) peeled and segmented
2 large oranges cut and sliced pith free.
30 black olives stoned
30 green olives stoned
1 red onion
 5 stalks of fresh mint (chopped) or dried mint (1tsp)
30ml (2tblsps) of sesame seeds
2.5ml (½ tsp) of cinnamon
15ml (1tblsp) red chilli flakes
25ml (1floz) extra virgin olive oil

**Take the cinnamon, chilli and olive oil and shake together. Mix all the rest to make the salad, lay it out and then add spicy oil at the last minute.**

An Eye For Good Food

# JEWELLED RICE SALAD

(Ian Grierson)

*A second salad that has origins from around the Middle East although I have eaten variations of this interestingly flavoured salad from as far away as Hong Kong.*

(For 6)

500g (1lb 2oz) brown rice (any rice will do except pudding rice)
Seeds of 1 pomegranate
50g (1 ¾ oz) dried cranberries
50g (1 ¾ oz) dried apricots (chopped)
50g (1 ¾ oz) sultanas
50g (1 ¾ oz) dried apple (chopped)
50g (1 ¾ oz) dried pineapple (chopped)
90ml (6tblsps) orange juice
30ml (2tblsps) fresh mint
90g (3oz) chopped flaked almonds

**Cook the rice for the required time (around 25 minutes). Place all the fruit when chopped up in the orange juice and any other juices from the pomegranate when the seeds are removed. Mix the fruit and juices through the rice when it is still warm but cooled down. Chop up the mint and almonds and spread them on the salad before serving (up to a day after).**

An Eye For Good Food

# TUNA & PASTA SALAD

(Ian Grierson)

*The Royal Hospital in Liverpool has a very reasonable salad bar at lunch time and of the various salads available, Tuna and Pasta is the favourite with most people. The pasta is always "Bows" which the Italians call "Farfalle" but the French have the best name - they call them " Papillons" (butterflies).*

**(4 persons)**

250g (8oz) of pasta bows
1 (200g) tin of tuna
1 (200g) tin of sweet corn
2 spring onions
45ml (3 tblsps) mayonnaise
30ml (2tblsps) plain yoghurt

**Cook the pasta bows in salted water for the time recommended on the packet and allow them to cool. Mix in the tuna, mayonnaise, sweet corn and chopped spring onions together and then fold carefully into the pasta and serve.**

# TUNA & AVOCADO SALAD

(Margaret Guppy from Liverpool for Bradbury Fields)

*Tuna and avocado are a good combination together and they do make a low GI salad with lots of goodness and micronutrients. The salad recipe of tuna and avocado has its origins in the Southern States of the USA where they would serve it with boiled eggs (as Margaret has got) and with lashings of mayo and hot sauce (Margaret has kept her version far healthier for us).*

**(Serves 4)**

198g (7oz) tin of tuna which is drained and flaked
1 whole lettuce
2 hard boiled eggs
2 ripe avocados, peeled, stoned and sliced
6 anchovy fillets (from a jar or tin)
30ml (2tblsps) of chopped chives for garnish

**DRESSING**
30ml (2tblsps) of lemon juice
15ml (1tblsp) of Dijon mustard
75ml (5tblsps) of virgin olive oil
5ml (1tsp) of honey
Pepper for seasoning

**Wash and separate the lettuce leaves then dry them and tear into pieces. Place the leaves on the base of a salad bowl. Top with chopped eggs, avocado and anchovies. Place the dressing in a screw top jar and shake to blend well pour the dressing over the salad and scatter on the chopped chives then serve.**

An Eye For Good Food

# POTATO SALAD WITH SAUSAGE

(Ian Grierson)

*There are variations of hot and cold salads that are based on potatoes and sausages from around the World and there are some very nice English ones. The present salad is Scandinavian and I think more specifically it is from southern Sweden but I have added a French dressing because the Scandinavian dressing takes no prisoners.*

**(A tasty and filling combination for 6)**

250g (nearly 9oz) large garlic sausage or even Spanish chiritzo sausage
1 onion
12 cherry tomatoes
10 small gherkins
300g (10oz) of boiled new potatoes
2 courgettes
5ml (1tsp) dried thyme (dried oregano will do)
5ml (1tsp) Dijon mustard
60ml (4tblsps) virgin olive oil
15ml (1tblsp) wine vinegar
30ml (2tblsp) olive oil for frying
Packet (120g) of mixed salad leaves (1 large packet or 2 small)

**Take the boiled potatoes when they are cold and slice into reasonable sized chunks and set aside. Heat up the 2 tblsps of olive oil in a pan, add in the chopped onion and sausage and cook for 3 minutes or so then introduced the chopped courgettes and the thyme for a further 2 minutes. Finally add in the halved tomatoes and sliced gherkins and mix. Add the mixture to the potatoes and as it is cooling down dress with the mixture of mustard, oil and vinegar. When cold spread on top of the salad leaves.**

# GREEN & RED SALAD

(Ian Grierson)

*For simplicity sake I have combined a standard green salad with a tomato salad and the dressing I suggest a simple Spanish vinaigrette.*

**(Salad for 6 or more)**

One standard lettuce
4 spring onions
½ a cucumber
½ a green pepper
6 tomatoes
3 radishes
6 mushrooms
1 lemon
125ml (5floz) virgin olive oil
2 cloves of garlic
5ml (1 tsp) dried parsley

**Wash and tear up the lettuce into a salad bowl, chop in the spring onion and green pepper, split the cucumber length wise and slice into ½ rings, slice tomatoes, slice radishes and raw mushrooms finely. Add each as layers ending up with tomatoes on top. Make the vinaigrette by chopping up the garlic cloves well, mixing in the dried parsley, squeeze in the lemon juice and add to oil –shake well and add half to the salad and reserve the rest for pouring when required.**

# NICOL'S SALAD

(Olga Valez from Woodford, Essex for WBPS)

*Olga says that she gave her son (Nicol) this salad on a regular basis because it is so tasty, nutritious and simple.*

**(For 2)**

3 regular tomatoes
6 medium sized mushrooms
15ml (1 tblsp) of lemon juice
45ml (3 tblsps) virgin olive oil (or walnut oil)

**Slice the tomatoes and mushrooms thinly and arrange them alternately round the plate. Mix the oil and lemon juice and drizzle on the salad and pepper well. Something interesting can go in the middle perhaps tuna, cooked chicken, a few prawns or some salad leaves perhaps?**

# BEAN SALAD

(Ian Grierson)

*A salad we use quite often on holidays because it is easy to put together, very nutritious and rather nice for a quick lunch. The salad is fine with most dressings but we tend to use pre-made Italian dressing.*

**(Lots for 4)**

Tin (400g) of red kidney beans
Tin (300g) of butter beans
1 jar (between 250 and 300g) of mixed mushrooms
275g (8oz) of fresh button mushrooms
Small (200g) tin of artichoke hearts
½ an onion
15ml (1tblsp) olive oil
½ a large bag or 1 small (60g) of mixed salad leaves

**Chop the fresh mushrooms and the onion and cook in a pan with the oil for no more than a minute then mix in the beans and jar of mushrooms and heat for a couple of minutes with gentle stirring to mix and heat evenly. Cool the mixture and chop up the artichoke hearts and mix in. Pour into a salad bowl with a base of mixed salad leaves. Add a dressing if required and most are suitable.**


# TOMATO, FETA & BASIL SALAD

(Dr Helen Orton from Liverpool for the Foundation)

*A simple but delicious salad that is highly nutritious. As I am writing this I am looking at a load of basil in the window and I know there are tomatoes and feta in our fridge – yum!*

**(4 people or small servings for 8)**

450g (1lb) of best quality vine tomatoes
150g (about 5oz) of feta cheese
30g (1oz) of fresh basil
30ml (2tblsps) virgin olive oil

**Slice the tomatoes horizontally and arrange in an oval shallow dish. Break up or cube the feta cheese and scatter over the tomatoes. Chop up the basil including stalks and spread over the salad and add some ground black pepper then drizzle over olive oil and eat right away.**

*An Eye For Good Food*

# SMOKED TROUT SALAD

(Maureen Frawley from Limerick, Ireland for the WSBPS)

*Maureen loves fish and salads and hopes the antioxidants, like those in this salad, will help slow down the progress of her Age-Related Macular Degeneration (AMD) but essentially it is a great summer salad.*

(Serves 4 for a meal and 6 as a starter)

8 boiled new potatoes
At least 200g (about 7oz) of smoked trout
2 hard boiled eggs
3 spring onions
2 tomatoes
Large bunch (200g) of watercress
15ml (1tblsp) Dijon mustard
60ml (4tblsps) olive oil
1 lemon
(Seasoning)

**Chop up the potatoes, eggs, spring onions and tomatoes, mix in a salad bowl, season with a little salt and black pepper and flake the trout into the salad. Drizzle over the dressing made from mustard, oil and lemon juice and serve out onto plates that have a scattering of watercress.**

# BEETROOT SALAD

(Gwendoline Grierson for the WSBPS)

*My mum absolutely loved fresh beetroot with mayonnaise or salad cream so every salad had to have both in it. Here is one she liked particularly because cheese was also a great favourite.*

(Lunch for 4)

4 cooked fresh beetroot
16 cherry tomatoes
½ a red onion
225g (½ lb) of Lancashire cheese
60ml (4tblsps) best mayonnaise

**Slice the beetroot, finely chop the onion and share these and the tomatoes between each of the plates. Crumble or grate the cheese on top and put a large dollop of mayonnaise on the side of each plate. Pepper the salad and serve up with fresh bread.**

An Eye For Good Food

# Main Courses

For our main courses we have vegetarian, fish, poultry and red meat based recipes. I think there is something for everyone some are classics and some a little more unusual.

An Eye For Good Food

**MAIN COURSES**

# HERBY POTATO BAKE

(Margaret Guppy from Liverpool for Bradbury Fields)

*It always amazes me how many ways there are to make potatoes spectacular and here is Margaret giving us another! I have put this as a main course because with a few vegetables on the side that is exactly what it is! Margaret says her potatoes go well with barbeque food and they can be served hot or cold.*

**(Serving for 2 and a meal for 1)**

2 large potatoes
30g (1oz) of butter
10ml (2tsps) of olive oil
15ml (1tblsp) of vegetable oil
1 bunch (125g) of spring onions
(Salt and pepper)
Dried or fresh chopped herbs that might include some or all of the following- rosemary, thyme, oregano and basil.

**Fry the sliced spring onions in the vegetable oil for 2 mins and remove from the heat. Wash the potatoes and cut them into quarters with their skins on. Butter a medium sized oven-proof dish and place half the potatoes in the dish adding a little extra butter, the onions and half of your herbs. Place the remaining potatoes on top of the onions mixed with the remaining herbs. Dot on the remaining butter and cover the dish with tin foil. Cook in a moderate oven (180°C) for 50 mins. Take out the dish remove the foil and put back in the oven for 10 mins browning.**

An Eye For Good Food

# MUSHROOM PIE

(Ian Grierson)

*I think this dish originates in the USA where they tend to call everything that involves the use of pastry as being a pie. However I think we would call this a pasty. Tart or pasty it is tasty and easy to make.*

**(For 4 on its own or 6 to 8 with salad)**

1 onion
5ml (1tsp) curry powder
400g (14oz) sliced mushrooms
500g (1lb 2oz) puff pastry
1 egg
60g (2oz) processed peas
60g (2oz) sweet corn

**Dice the onion up finely and fry in the sunflower oil adding in the curry powder for 2 minutes and then add in the sliced mushrooms and cook for a further 2 minutes. Take off the heat and add in all the peas and corn and mix well. Roll out the pastry into a rectangle and cut into two. Add the mixture to the centre of one and brush the edge with egg. Place on the top and pinch closed. Cook at 200°C for no more than 20 minutes and allow to cool. Slice the pie into 4 or 8.**

# CAULIFLOWER & LENTIL CURRY

(Margaret Guppy from Liverpool for Bradbury Fields)

*If you think vegetables are boring then try this extremely tasty vegetable curry from Margaret – also Dee tells me that lentils are a highly nutritious GI food.*

**(For at least 4 as main dish and 6 as a side dish)**

1 cauliflower chopped into small pieces
25ml (1 floz) vegetable oil
100g (3 ½ oz) of parboiled lentils (chana dhall)
2 medium onions finely chopped
2.5ml (½ tsp) salt
2.5ml (½ tsp) of mild chilli powder
2.5ml (½ tsp) of turmeric
2.5ml (½ tsp) of coriander
2.5ml (½ tsp) of ground cumin
30ml (2 tblsps) of desiccated coconut
Juice of 1 lemon

**Fry the onions in oil for 4 mins gently then add cauliflower, lentils, all the spices, coconut and salt. Add two cups of water and cook on a low heat until the cauliflower is tender but still together then add lemon juice. The total cooking time should be around 30 mins.**

An Eye For Good Food

# GREEN BEANS with TOMATO & GARLIC SAUCE

(Margaret Guppy from Liverpool for Bradbury Fields)

*Margaret suggests that you either use one bean of your choice or as she prefers a mixture of beans. The bean stew can act as a main course and goes well with rice I think or with a smaller portion and the addition of some grilled meat or fish can appeal to carnivores as well.*

**(4 as mains or 6 as a side dish with meat)**

675g (1 ½ lb) of mixed green beans (French, broad, runner or dwarf all work)
15ml (1tblsp) of sunflower oil
1 medium onion peeled and finely chopped
2 cloves of garlic peeled and crushed
400g (14oz) tin of chopped tomatoes
(salt and pepper)
2.5ml ( ½ tsp) dry or 5ml (1 tsp) fresh oregano
5ml (1tsp) of sugar

**Trim the beans and cook them in a pan of boiling water for about 8 mins. Meanwhile heat the oil in the pan and fry the onion and garlic for about 5 mins until the onions begin to soften. Add in the contents of the tin of tomatoes and continue to cook until the liquid starts to thicken, season and sprinkle in the oregano and sugar. Drain the beans placing them in a serving dish and pour over the tomato sauce and serve at once.**

An Eye For Good Food

**MAIN COURSES**

# VEGETABLE CHILLI

(Jane Sedgwick from Upton for the WSBPS)

*Have most of your five portions at one sitting with this healthy but tasty vegetable dish.*

**(Serves 4)**

½ a large cauliflower or a whole small one
1 courgette
1 onion
1 red or green pepper
½ a turnip (Swede)
4 large carrots
250g (8oz) of mushrooms
5ml (1tsp) paprika
5-10ml (1-2tsps) chilli powder according to strength and taste
15ml (1tblsp) of flour
30ml (2tblsps) tomato puree or more
1 tin (440g) of plum tomatoes
30ml (2tblsps) sunflower oil

Slice up all the vegetables and first fry off the chopped onion in oil until soft. Add paprika, chilli and flour and coat all the onions then take off the heat. Take two generous tblsps of tomato puree and in a measuring jug mix with ¾ pt of boiling water stirring well. Now and this liquid and the tin of tomatoes to the onions and break up the tomatoes a little. Finally add in all the chopped vegetables, bring to the boil and simmer for 30 mins. Transfer to an oven proof dish and cook for an hour at 180°C. Serve up a generous ladle of vegetables with roast potatoes sprinkled with rosemary.

# VEGETABLE AU GRATIN

(Margaret Guppy from Liverpool for Bradbury Fields)

*Another recipe that puts a little bit more flavour into a dish with plenty of healthy vegetables.*

**(Plenty for 6)**

15ml (1tblsp) vegetable oil
30g (1oz) of butter
1 medium onion chopped
1 crushed clove of garlic
450g (1lb) of sliced young carrots
450g (1lb) of sliced courgettes
(Salt and pepper)
450 (1lb) of tomatoes skinned and sliced

## TOPPING

40g (1 ½ oz) of butter
40g (1 ½ oz) of plain flour
450ml (¾ pt) of milk
(Salt and pepper)
5ml (1tsp) of Dijon mustard
2.5ml (½ tsp) of ground nutmeg
1 egg beaten
90g (3oz) of grated strong Cheddar cheese

**Heat the oil and butter in a pan and add in the onions, garlic, carrots and fry them gently for 10 mins. Increase the heat and add the courgettes frying them for 5 mins. Season and turn into a large but shallow oven proof dish and cover with sliced tomato. For the topping heat the butter in a pan then add the flour and cook for 1 min and then gradually blend in the milk bringing to the boil. Add the seasoning, nutmeg and mustard before removing the pan from the heat and stirring in the beaten egg and half the cheese and finally pour the sauce over the vegetables. Sprinkle the remaining cheese on top of the dish and place on a baking dish in the oven at 200°C for 20 mins.**

An Eye For Good Food

# SAVOURY BREAD & BUTTER PUDDING

(Margaret Guppy from Liverpool for Bradbury Fields)

*An unusual dish that is certainly worth a try and Margaret says it is "Ideal with salad".*

**(Plenty for 4)**

6 slices of white buttered bread with the crusts cut off
180g (6oz) of strong grated Cheddar cheese
1 large onion, peeled and finely chopped
3 large eggs
650ml (1¼ pts) of warmed but not overly hot milk
1.25ml (¼ tsp) Dijon mustard
(Salt and pepper)

Grease a medium sized oven proof dish. Lightly fry the chopped onion for 3 mins. Remove from heat and drain on kitchen roll. Keep 25g (1oz) of cheese to the side then mix the bulk of the cheese, onion and mustard together. Place half the bread, butter side up, on the base of the dish. Add in ¾ of the cheesy mixture onto the bread then add in the remaining bread also butter side up. Finally top with the remaining cheese mix. Beat your eggs, pour in the warm milk and lightly season before whisking all together lightly. Pour the milk and eggs into the dish and leave to settle for 10 to 15 mins. Place the dish in the pre-heated oven at 180°C for 25 mins then remove from the oven and sprinkle on the rest of the cheese and return to the oven for a last 10 mins to let the top brown a little.

# NOODLES & PRAWNS

(Dr Robert Ritch from New York for the Foundation)

*It is best to do this dish in a wok or a very large frying pan. Dr Ritch says the secret is to have everything at hand and serve hot to the table but I can assure you this is a magnificently flavoursome and nutritious dish – all the flavours of the Far East.*

### (Serves 4)

1 pre-cooked chicken breast – chopped fine or shredded
3 cloves of garlic minced
1 onion chopped fine
12 large peeled fresh prawns
450g (1lb) freshly cooked Chinese noodles
300g (2/3rds lb) of broccoli (chopped) or thin purple sprouting broccoli or bok choi
150g (4 ½ oz) of fresh bean sprouts
60g (2oz) roasted peanuts (crushed)
4 spring onions (chopped)
650ml (1 ¼ pts) of chicken stock
30ml (2 tblsps) of soy sauce
5ml (1 tsp) of fish sauce
1 chopped tomato
15ml (1 tblsp) of chilli sauce
2 eggs slightly beaten
30ml (2tblsps) of peanut oil

**Add the oil to the wok and partly cook the prawns until they just change colour and remove. Stir fry the garlic, onion and broccoli for a couple of minutes then add in the eggs and let the egg cook for a minute. Toss in the tomato and sauces, the prawns again (if precooked prawns then add them here also) then finish with bean sprouts before adding in the stock mixing well and bringing up to heat.**

**Have the noodles cooking in boiling water at the same time as stir frying. When done drain and split them between the four bowls. Some stir fry on top and then sprinkle on the cold shredded chicken, onion and the nuts.**

MAIN COURSES

An Eye For Good Food

# FAST FISH PIE

(Lindy Gee from Wirral for the Foundation)

*Lindy is the PA for one of the Eye professors in Liverpool University and says that her fish pie is very simple, quick to make and should be enjoyed with a dry white wine. I do love fish pie and all that omega-3 is so good for you!*

**(for 4 people)**

200g (6 ½ oz) of fresh salmon
200g (6 ½ oz) of white fish (smoked or fresh)
1K (2.2lbs) of potatoes
200g (6 ½ oz) of frozen peas
160g ( just over 5oz) of mature cheddar
45g (1.5oz) of butter
30ml (2 tblsps) of milk
2.5ml ( ½ tsp) of vegetable oil
(Salt and pepper)

Take an ovenproof dish and rub it out with the oil to prevent the fish from sticking. Place the fish into the dish and cover them with milk (about 30ml or so), salt and pepper as required. Preheat oven to 1800C. In the mean time peel and boil the potatoes in salted water for 20 minutes. While the potatoes are boiling put the fish and milk into the oven to cook for the 20 minutes also. Gently cook the frozen peas in a small pan making sure they do not boil and grate your cheese. When the fish is cooked everything else should be ready. Take the fish out of the oven and drain off the milk and reserve; chop up the fish to small pieces if needed. Put the oven up to 220°C. Add butter to the potatoes and any seasoning then mash finely using the reserved fish milk to help. When finished fold in the cooked peas to the mash and layer with a fork the mixture on top of the fish spreading evenly. Spread the cheese on top and leave in the oven for 20 minutes turning the pie once during this time.

An Eye For Good Food

# DOUBLE FISH PIE

(Margaret Guppy from Liverpool for Bradbury Fields)

*We had several fish pie recipes submitted so it only seemed right to have a second one in the book. Try them both Dee and I have and can thoroughly recommend them to you!*

**(For 4 or more)**

350g (12oz) of cod or whiting
350g (12oz) of smoked fish
600ml (1pt 2floz) of milk
60g (2oz) of butter
60g (2oz) of plain flour
175g (6oz) button mushrooms that need sliced up
Freshly ground black pepper

**TOPPING**
450g (1lb) of potatoes
Enough butter and milk for mashing
100g (3 ½ oz) mature cheddar cheese that's been grated
(Season to taste)

**Boil the potatoes until tender. Meanwhile put the milk in a pan with the fish and simmer gently for 10 mins. Strain and reserve the milk and flake the fish with a fork removing bit bits of skin and any bones. Leave the fish on one side. Melt the butter in a pan and add the flour stirring gently for 1 min. Then gradually add in the reserved milk a little at a time; keep stirring until the sauce is nice and thick. Add in the chopped mushrooms and flaked fish with a little seasoning (Margaret adds a splash of lemon juice at this stage as an option). Turn the mixture into a 1.75L (3pt) oven proof dish. Drain the potatoes and mash with some butter and milk and stir in ¾ rs of the cheese and season. Spread the potato evenly over the fish mixture and decorate with a fork. Sprinkle the remaining cheese on top of the potato and put dish in the oven at 200°C. After 30 to 40 mins the pie will be ready and the top will be golden brown – serve at once.**

MAIN COURSES

An Eye For Good Food

# KIPPER TART

(Ian Grierson)

*Kippers are so underrated and, for fish these days, inexpensive. Smoked mackerel works just as well and doesn't need cooking so it is simpler. To make the tart as simple as possible I recommend supermarket pastry cases but your own would be better if you have the mind. The tart goes very well with whole potatoes or salad.*

**(For 4 people)**

2 fresh (350g) kippers or boil in the bag ones are fine
1 shop bought, short crust pastry case (savoury)
½ lemon
275 ml ( ½ pt) of skimmed milk
3 large eggs
10ml (2tsps) of English mustard
1.23ml (¼ tsp) of nutmeg
5ml (1tsp) of black pepper

**Grill the kippers for 3 minutes on each side or boil in the bag for the time recommended. Set aside or remove from the bag and allow to cool. Skin the fish and flake removing bones. Egg wash the pastry case and then layer the fish over the case with a squeeze of lemon juice. Whisk the milk with 2 eggs, the mustard and nutmeg and pour mixture over the fish. Put pie case on a heated baking sheet in the middle of the oven at 190°C and bake for 40 minutes by which time the filling should be golden. The tart needs a few minutes resting and can be eaten hot or cold.**

# BAKED TROUT

(Hazel Rushton from Northwich, Cheshire for the Foundation)

*Trout used at one time to be a rare treat now they are, in the form of rainbow trout, readily available being a successfully farmed fish. I'm not sure why they are not more popular than they are and I believe many people have not ever tried them. Here is your chance with a very good trout dish. Hazel says that this is an easy recipe and the fish is ready in 50 minutes.*

**(2 people. And candlelight, perhaps?)**

1 lemon thinly sliced
2 handfuls (about 50g) of button mushrooms cut in half
2 fennel bulbs thinly sliced
2 whole trout (they need gutted and cleaned which the fishmonger will do)
A bunch of tarragon (chops down to 30ml (2tbls))
2 shallots finely sliced
30ml (2 tblsps) of white wine
60gm (2oz) of butter

**Heat the oven to 200ºC and line a shallow roasting tin or dish with excess baking paper (enough to wrap up the fish) on which make a bed of thin sliced fennel. Sit the cleaned trout on top and stuff the remaining fennel the shallot and the tarragon into the fish cavities then top with lemon slices and mushrooms. Dot the fish with butter and pour in the wine. Fold up the paper to make a loose enclosed parcel then bake for 30 minutes. Enjoy with some roast potatoes or rice perhaps?**

# SALMON EN CROUTE

(Heather Sutton from Knutsford, Cheshire for the Foundation)

*Heather is a fund raiser for the Foundation for Prevention of Blindness and now we know she cooks recipes like this then Dee and I will be finding lame excuses to invite ourselves over to her house preferably around dinner time!*

**(Serves at least 2)**

150g (5oz) of mascarpone or cream cheese
120g (4oz) bag of watercress, spinach and rocket
500g (1lb+) of short crust pastry (use butter version)
500g (1lb +) of skinless salmon fillet(s)
1 beaten egg

**Heat oven to 200°C and put the mascarpone and salad leaves into a food processor and whizz to a creamy green puree that requires seasoning.**

# APRICOT & LAMB BUTTERFLIES

(Margaret Guppy from Liverpool for Bradbury Fields)

*Lamb (like duck) and fruit go well together and apricot and lamb are extremely good partners. They are a common combination in French cuisine and even more frequent in North African cooking. You might not get double loin chops from the supermarket but any good butcher will cut them for you.*

**(Serves 4)**

4 lamb butterfly or Barnsley chops (double loin chops)
1 large tin (600g) of apricot halves
5ml (1tsp) of arrowroot powder
5ml (1tsp) of mustard
15ml (1tblsp) of clear honey
15ml (1tblsp) of lemon juice
4 sprigs of rosemary for garnish

**Bake the chops in a roasting tin in the oven at 200°C for around 30 mins until cooked. Drain the apricots chop them coarsely but reserve 200ml (7 fl oz) of the juice from the tin. Blend arrowroot and mustard into the juice and pour over the chopped apricots in a pan and stir well adding in the lemon juice and honey. Cook over a gentle heat stirring continuously until the sauce thickens and clears a bit. Serve the chops coated with the apricot sauce and a sprig of rosemary on each plate. The dish will go well with new potatoes, mash or rice. We tried it with pasta and it was great!**

# SALMON & CUCUMBER SAUCE

(Teri Holmes from Wirral for the WSBPS)

*Salmon is so readily available, reasonably priced and full of good fats like the omega 3 fatty acids – we all should eat more of it and here is an excellent recipe with a sauce that totally complements the fish.*

(Portions for 2)

2 salmon steaks
½ a cucumber
30g (1 oz) of plain flour
30g (1 oz) of butter
225ml (½ pt) of milk
½ a lemon
45ml (3 tblsps) of single cream
(Salt and pepper)

Cook the salmon any way you wish but Terri suggests 5 mins in the microwave at full power is sufficient. Peel the cucumber and slice it along its length and remove the wet seedy part. Chop up the flesh and then cook the cucumber in melted butter in a pan for 5 mins. Sprinkle in the flour while stirring and then add the milk gradually and bring to the boil continuing to stir all the time. Season and simmer for between 2 and 3 mins then introduce the lemon juice off the heat and finally stir in the cream also off the heat and serve over the salmon. This dish I think goes well with mash or sauté potatoes.

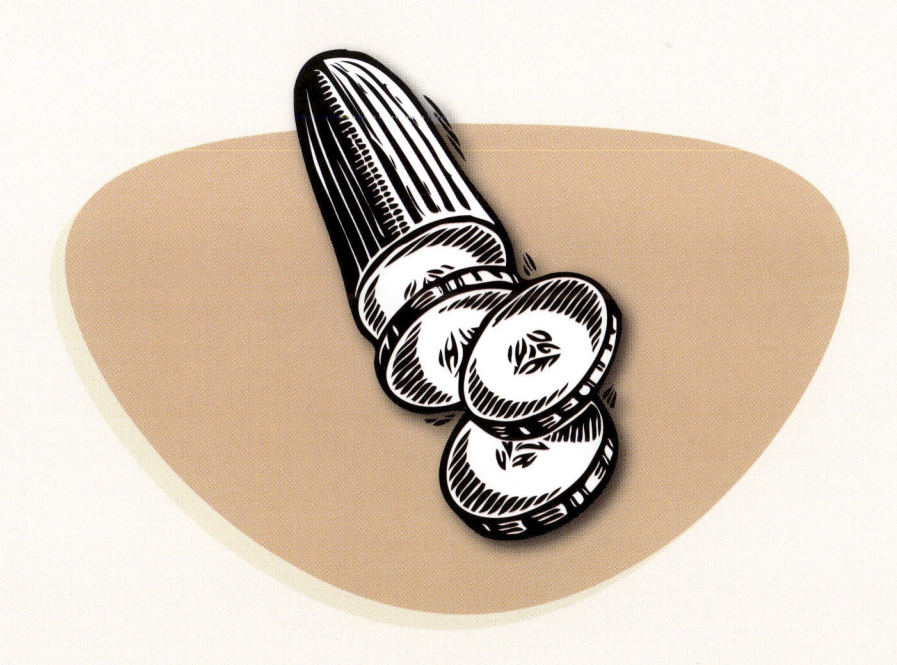

MAIN COURSES

An Eye For Good Food

# COQ-AU-VIN

(Trevor Holland from Windermere Manor Hotel for WBPS)

*Trevor says that his Coq-au-Vin recipe tastes even better if you have a view of Lake Windermere but I'm sure it is great where ever you are!*

**(For 1)**

1 clove of garlic crushed
2 chicken legs skinned
15g ( ½ oz) of butter
15ml (1tblsp) oil
12 button mushrooms
8 baby onions
15g ( ½ oz) of plain flour
150ml (6 floz)of red wine
75ml (3 floz) of chicken stock
1 bouquet garni
2.5ml (½ tsp) of brown sugar
Fresh parsley to taste

**Heat the butter in a frying pan and brown the chicken on both sides. Place the joints in a casserole dish. Fry onions and mushrooms in the frying pan for 3 minutes and pass them over into the casserole. Mix the flour in with the butter juices and separate the bits off the bottom of the pan. Add in the wine slowly stirring continuously until the lumps have been removed then add the stock, bouquet garni, sugar, garlic and season with salt and pepper if you wish. Pour mixture over the chicken and cover the dish with silver foil and cook for 30 minutes at 180°C. Remove bouquet garni, garnish with plenty of chopped parsley and serve with potatoes and vegetables.**

# CHICKEN & LEEK PIE

(Nadeen Jennings from Wavertree, Liverpool for the Foundation)

*Chicken and leeks work very well together and they are, as I remember, the key ingredients of St David's stew but here Nadeen Jennings has worked them into a very flavoursome and nutritious pie.*

**(For 2 people)**

75ml (3 floz) of dry white wine
200ml (7 floz) of chicken stock
1 bay leaf
1 garlic clove
2 medium leeks (washed trimmed of the hardest green leaves and sliced to 1 cm chunks)
450g (1lb) of boneless, skinless chicken portions (thighs?) sliced up
30g (1oz) of butter
30ml (2 tblsps) of plain flour
100ml (4 floz) of double cream
3 big sprigs of tarragon (leaves only)
5ml (1tsp) Dijon mustard
30g (1oz) or 2 handfuls of grated mature cheddar
(seasoning)
225g ( ½ lb) of decent puff pastry (all butter)
1 beaten egg

**Put wine and stock in a saucepan with the bay leaf and garlic. Bring to the simmer and add the leeks with the chicken on top. Return to simmer and cook for 15 minutes or until the chicken is cooked. Strain liquid into a jug and place to one side. Remove the chicken and leeks and allow to cool. On a floured surface roll out your pastry to about ½ cm thick and 3cm longer than your pie dish. Cut a 1cm strip long enough to go round the wet rim of the dish then lay the crust over the top. Make a couple of holes for steam and flute the edge with a fork to make a decent seal. Chill the pie in the fridge for 20 minutes, brush the pastry with egg wash and cook in the oven at 200°C for 25 minutes until the pie is risen and golden.**

An Eye For Good Food

# CHICKEN WITH LETTUCE SAUCE

(Terri Holmes from Wirral for the WSBPS)

*Chicken joints can be a little boring sometimes but not when you have livened them up with a tasty marinade and an interesting sauce.*

(Plenty for 4)

8 chicken drumsticks or thighs

### MARINADE
75ml (5tblsps) of olive oil
Juice of 1 lemon
15ml (1tblsp) of chopped fresh chervil
(Salt and black pepper)

### SAUCE
60g (2oz) unsalted butter
1 bunch of chopped spring onions
1 Cos lettuce
45ml (3 tblsps) of white wine
30ml (2 tblsps) of crème fraiche
15ml (1 tblsp) of chopped fresh chervil

**Cut the skin of the chicken joints and marinate in the mixture of chervil, oil and lemon in either a bowl or in a sealed polythene bag in the fridge for at least 2 hrs and best overnight. Grill the joints for 12 to 15 mins, turning and basting with marinade. For your sauce, first melt the butter in a pan on low heat and cook chopped onions until soft then add in the torn up lettuce coating it with butter and finally introduce the wine and simmer for 5 to 7 mins. Remove from the heat and whizz in a food processor adding in the chervil and the crème fraiche. Serve the sauce with the chicken on a bed of rice or couscous.**

# CHICKEN & PARMA HAM

(Kathy Cracknell from Wales for the Foundation)

*Kathy got her PhD in 2008 and is a research worker in the Eye Research Group at Liverpool.*

(For 4)

4 chicken breasts
4 slices of Parma ham
45ml (3 tblsps) of garlic and herb soft cheese
20 cherry tomatoes
A splash of balsamic vinegar

**Cut a pocket along the length of each chicken breast and stuff the pocket with 2 teaspoons of the cream cheese, Wrap each chicken breast with a slice of Parma ham so that it holds the pocket shut. Place the chicken on a baking tray with the pocket facing up. Bake at 190°C for 20 minutes adding in the tomatoes to the baking tray 5 minutes before the end. Remove the chicken and serve it with the tomatoes on cous cous or with rice. Mix the balsamic with the juices in the baking tray over low heat making a gravy to pour over the meat.**

# PORK SHOULDER WITH CIDER

(Grace Greenhough, Cheshire for the Foundation)

*Pork and apple is such a good combination and here the apple is heightened by the presence of cider.*

(Plenty for 4)

1 (180g) jar of Bramley apple sauce
5ml (1tsp) of olive oil
5ml (1tsp) of butter
1 medium onion chopped
450g (1lb) of shoulder of pork
225ml ( ½ lb) of dry cider
35ml (1 ½ fl oz) cider vinegar
Seasoning

**Pre-heat the oven to 170°C then cut the pork into cubes. Heat the oil and butter in an oven proof pan or casserole dish and cook the onion for 5 minutes. Add in the pork increasing the heat and colour a little for a couple of minutes. Introduce the cider, vinegar and some seasoning and bring to simmering before putting in the oven without a lid for 1 hour. Stir in the apple sauce and crème fraiche and return to the oven for a final 15 minutes. Grace suggests serving up with new potatoes, chives, some spinach and a squeeze of lemon.**

**MAIN COURSES**

# SPICY CITRUS CHICKEN

(Judy Hollings from Cardiff, Wales for the Foundation)

*Judy has this tasty, fruity and very healthy chicken dish that ticks several boxes for inclusion in our book but as Judy is Professor Simon Harding's Mum who is the Chairman of the Foundation she doesn't really need them!*

**(Serves 4)**

15ml (1tblsp) plain flour
2.5ml (½ tsp) each of ground coriander, ground cumin and fresh pepper
4 chicken breast fillets or skinned chicken thighs
15ml (1tblsp) vegetable oil
Grated rind and juice of 1 orange
Grated rind and juice of 1 lime
10ml (2tsps) clear honey
1 onion finely chopped
225g (½ lb) of split red lentils
550ml (1pt) of chicken stock

**Place the flour, cumin, coriander and pepper in a polythene bag and then add the chicken and shake to give an even coating. Heat the oil in a frying pan and cook the coated chicken gently for 4 minutes turning once. Then add in any remaining spice mixture the fruit rind and juice and the honey. Bring up to the boil, cover and simmer for 15 minutes until the chicken is tender. Test the thickest part of the meat with a skewer, the juices should run clear. Meanwhile place the onions, lentils and stock in a saucepan, cover and cook gently for about 25 minutes by which time the stock will be absorbed. Arrange the lentils around a warm serving dish with the chicken in the centre. Pour sauce over and garnish with fresh coriander and some twists of orange and lime. Judy says brown rice or pasta will work just as well as lentils.**

An Eye For Good Food

# MEXICAN CASSEROLE

(Tracy Hill from Everton for the Foundation)

*An enjoyable taste of Mexico made easy by Tracy with a few tins of soup from the store cupboard. When I made it I used 1 tin of double thickness (diluting) soup (but didn't add water) and 1 tin of mushroom soup but it's up to you.*

(Plenty for 4)

1 chicken cooked and cut up into pieces. (450g (1lb) of beef mince will do also)
1 medium packet of tortilla chips
¼ onion (chopped)
¼ chopped green pepper
5ml (1tsp) chilli powder
2.5ml (½ tsp) garlic powder
15ml (1tlblsp) olive oil
2 tins (2x 400g) of chicken soup
1 tin (400g) of mushroom soup

**Warm the oil in a pan and add in the chopped onion, pepper, chilli and garlic and cook off for 2 minutes at low heat. Add in the soup and chopped chicken and warm up gently but don't boil stir in well. Serve in bowls with tortilla chips on the side.**

MAIN COURSES

An Eye For Good Food

**MAIN COURSES**

# CURRIED DUCK

(Dr Robert Ritch from New York for the Foundation)

*Curried duck is a spectacular dish and well worth the effort so do try this one if you can.*

**(Lots for 8 people)**

2 medium sizes ducks (around 4lbs each) – get them jointed with breasts, legs and wings removed
2 garlic cloves
1 carrot
1 stalk of celery
1 smashed stalk of lemon grass
1 bay leaf

### CURRY

2 chopped onions
6 chopped shallots (small onions)
6 garlic cloves chopped
1 inch of ginger (peeled)
5ml (1tsp) saffron
5ml (1tsp) salt
15ml (1tblsp) of good curry powder or paste
15ml (1tblsp) of olive oil
1 apple remove the seeds but do not peel
1 banana; peeled and cut into 6 pieces
5ml (1tsp) of star anise

2 smashed stalks of lemon grass
100ml (4 floz) of brandy
275ml (½ pt) of dry white wine
2 tomatoes coarsely chopped
1L (1 ¾ pts) of chicken broth
8 okra (ladies fingers) or green beans
4 small courgettes cut into discs
8 spring onions
(Black pepper for seasoning)
30ml (2tblsps) of tinned coconut milk

**Make a broth out of the duck trimmings and giblets by browning them in a pan and then adding 6 cups of water, 2 cloves of garlic, celery, carrot, lemon grass, bay leaf and simmer for 2 hrs. Add a little extra water if needed to barely cover the trimmings, strain and reserve.**

**Place onions, shallots, 4 cloves of garlic, chopped ginger and saffron into a food processor and blitz into a paste. Mix curry and salt (don't need this if using paste) and rub onto duck meat then brown off in olive oil adding breasts skin side down only for 5mins. Drain most of the fat from the pan, add pureed vegetables and cook under low heat, stirring a lot to prevent any burning for about 5 mins then add in chopped apple, banana, anise, crushed lemon grass and cook with stirring for a further 7 mins. To the fairly dry mix add duck, all remaining curry, the wine and brandy and the chopped tomatoes and cook for 10 mins, introduce the duck and chicken stock and simmer for 20 mins. Add okra, spring onions and courgettes and remove the spring onions and courgettes after 10 mins simmering. Cook the duck for a further 20 mins then remove it and put the duck with the onions and courgettes warming.**

**Return the okra and vegetable sauce to the heat and adjust taste with seasoning and additional curry powder (paste) if needed and simmer for 5 mins. Dr Ritch recommends that you take the thick coconut milk from the top of the tin and whisk into the sauce now off the heat. Ladle sauce over the duck and vegetables and serve up with boiled rice.**

An Eye For Good Food

# STIR FRY TURKEY

(Lynda Sedgewick from Wirral for the WSBPS)

*Lynda says this is one of her favourite mid-week meals. She says "it is easy, healthy and very tasty" and I'm sure you will agree with her once you have tried this recipe.*

(Serves 4)

275g (10oz) boneless raw turkey cut into bit-sized pieces
30ml (2tblsps) soy sauce
15ml (1tblsp) sherry or water
2.5ml (½ tsp) of dried ginger
10ml (2tsps) cornflour
10ml (2tsps) vegetable oil
3 spring onions trimmed and sliced
100g (3 ½ oz) chopped mushrooms
½ small or ¼ large cauliflower (10 florets or so)
60ml (4tblsps) of chicken or vegetable stock
Salt

**Mix the soy sauce, sherry, ginger and cornflour in a bowl then add in the turkey pieces coating them evenly. Heat 1 tblsp of oil in a large frying pan or wok over moderate heat until hot then stir fry the meat moving constantly for 1 minute. Transfer to a plate and keep warm in oven or grill. Heat the remaining oil and stir fry the vegetables for 3 minutes. Return chicken to the wok, season and fry for 1 more minute. Serve at once with rice.**

An Eye For Good Food

**MAIN COURSES**

# TAGIATELLI WITH PESTO & BACON

(Sue Hadley from Wirral for the WSBPS)

*Sue is the Chairperson of the Wirral Society of the Blind and Partly Sighted. To me she is always training or running in Marathons to raise money for a new extension to the Society's building. I'm therefore not surprised that Sue has given us a pasta recipe because pasta dishes are the athlete's favourite food because they top up energy reserves. We could all benefit from a bit of extra energy especially when the recipe is as Sue says "very tasty and very quick!"*

(Serves 2)

100g ( 3 ½ oz) of smoked back bacon (chopped)
15ml (1tblsp) pine nuts
50g (2 oz) of sun dried tomatoes from a delicatessen counter (chopped)
150g (6 oz) of fresh tagliatelle
30ml (2 tblsps) green pesto
30 ml (2tblsps) crème fraiche

**Dry fry the bacon for 4-5 minutes until it is crisp. Add in pine nuts and the dried tomatoes and cook for a further 1-2 minutes. Stir in pesto and crème fraiche and the sauce is ready. Meanwhile cook the fresh pasta for 4 minutes, drain and mix with your sauce – eat hot!**

An Eye For Good Food

# BACON & EGG PIE

(Ian Grierson)

*Of the various dishes we had for the soup and salad day at the WSBPS this bacon and egg pie was one of the favourites. I made three huge ones and they were gone in no time. Bacon and egg pie is rarely seen these days but is a British classic of the past. I always use readymade pastry and short crust rather than puff pastry although in New Zealand, where egg and bacon pie is an institution, puff pastry is usual.*

(Around 8 slices)

Readymade short crust pastry (circles if you can get them, you will need 2)
6 slices of smoked back bacon
15ml (1tblsp) of vegetable oil
2 boiled and sliced potatoes
4 eggs
10ml (2tsps) of milk
(Seasoning)

**Boil one of the eggs and let it cool. Fry the bacon gently for a few mins in a pan so that it is lightly cooked, remove cut into pieces and reserve. Slice the potato and sauté to light brown in the same pan. Roll one circle out a little bit more and fit it into a large circular but shallow pie (quiche) tin making sure the pastry goes up the sides to the top. Scatter bacon and fried potato on the base then slices of boiled egg. Lightly beat the 3 remaining eggs pour on top, season with pepper and place second pastry circle on top trimming the lid to a slight overlap. Crimp edges with your fingers and lightly brush with milk to seal. Bake in the middle of the oven at 200°C for 15 mins then turn the heat down to 1800C for around 45 mins when golden brown. Allow the pie to cool and serve up slices with salad for a filling main meal.**

An Eye For Good Food

# SCOUSE

(Karen Tynan from Everton for the Foundation)

*A recipe book sponsored by 3 Merseyside organisations needs to have a good Scouse recipe and the one sent in by Karen fits the bill very well!*

(Serves 4 to 6 people)

225g (½ lb) of stewing steak
225g (½ lb) of lamb's breast
1 large onion (chopped)
450g (1lb) of carrots
2 ¼ Kg (5lbs) of potatoes
2 beef stock cubes
10ml (2tsps) of vegetable oil
Worcestershire sauce
Water and seasoning

**Cut all the meat into large cubes and fry in vegetable oil until lightly browned; some Worcestershire sauce at this stage adds flavour. Transfer meat to a large saucepan and add the onion and carrot with 1lb of the diced potatoes on top of the carrots. Add cold water until the pan is half full and then break up the stock cubes and add some seasoning. Let the pan simmer gently and give the odd stir. Simmer for two hours then add the remaining potatoes as the original ones will have broken up and add a few splashes of Worcester sauce and simmer for two more hours.**

**Serve hot with red cabbage, beetroot, pickled onions and crusty bread.**

# PORK CHOP & CIDER CASSEROLE

(Margaret Guppy from Liverpool for Bradbury Fields)

*Similar dish to the last and just as nice but with a remarkably different flavour – try them both if you don't believe me!*

**(Serves 4)**

4 pork chops
15ml (1tblsp) vegetable or olive oil
1 medium onion sliced
15g (½ oz) seasoned flour
5ml (1 tsp) or more of chopped fresh sage or 2.5ml (½ tsp) of dried sage
150ml (about ¼ pt) of vegetable stock
150ml (about ¼ pt) of dry cider
2 apples peeled and cored

**Place the chops in hot oil in a heavy frying pan and brown both sides, after 5 mins introduce chopped onions and after 10 mins remove chops and onions with slotted spoon into a 3 pt casserole dish. Drain off most of the fat from the frying pan and add flour stirring gently for 1 min. Add the sage, the stock and cider stirring continuously until the liquid comes to the boil. Then pour the liquid over the chops and cook in the oven at 160°C for 1 hour. Peel, core and chop apples, introduce to the casserole and continue cooking for a further 15 mins then serve with potatoes and vegetables or rice and vegetables.**

# COTTAGE PIE

(Doreen Ryan from Woolton for the Foundation)

*I cannot think of anything nicer to come home to on a wet and blustery day than cottage pie. It is real comfort food and all you need is a fork –and a nice glass of wine perhaps?*

**(Serves 6)**

45ml (3tblsps) olive oil
1 large onion (chopped)
2 sticks of celery (finely chopped)
2 carrots diced finely
3 cloves of garlic finely chopped
675g (1 ½ lb) minced beef (or lamb to make shepherd's pie version)
15ml (1tblsp) tomato puree
3-4 drops of Worcestershire sauce
3-4 drops of Tabasco sauce
175ml (6 floz) of dry white or red wine
300ml (over ½ pt) of chicken stock
(Seasoning)

## TOPPING
1.4g potatoes
50ml (2 floz) of milk
30ml (2 tblsps) mature Cheddar cheese
15ml (1 tblsp) finely grated Parmesan

**Heat oven to 180°C. Heat oil in a large frying pan and add the onion, celery and carrot and after 5 minutes add the garlic and soften everything on low heat. Add the mince and increase the heat stirring until browned, Then stir in the tomato puree, the sauces, wine and stock, season, cover and simmer for 10 minutes. At the same time boil the potatoes in salted water until soft and mash with the milk until the potato is smooth and creamy. Spoon the mince into a gratin dish and cover with a thick even layer of potato. Sprinkle on all the cheese and bake for 40-55 minutes until gold and bubbling and serve up with seasonal vegetables.**

An Eye For Good Food

# MEATY BOLOGNAISE

(Jaqui from Dubai for the WSBPS)

*Spaghetti bolognaise when the sauce is nice, meaty and substantial is very much an English take on the original Italian where the sauce is very thin. Here is a really substantial sauce – I'm not sure how well it goes down in Dubai but it works wonders in a cold North West of England winter.*

**(Fine for 6 people)**

1 onion
1 garlic clove
15ml (1tblsp) olive oil
1 carrot
1 stick of celery
90g (3 oz) of mushrooms (chopped)
90g (3 oz) green bacon (chopped)
Minced beef (large pack around 675g (1 ½ lb))
275ml ( ½ pt) of red wine
60ml (4 tblsps) of tomato puree
275ml ( ½ pt) of beef stock (by stock cube if you wish)
15-30ml (1-2tblsps) of double cream
15g (1tblsp) of grated cheese (optional)

**Add oil to the pan, chop all the vegetables and cook for 5 minutes until soft. Add in the bacon and mince and brown off for couple of minutes. Moisten with the wine and simmer for 2 minutes. Add reasoning, tomato puree and the stock and cook for 1 ½ hours and at the end stir in the cream and mix in well. Serve with pasta or rice and sprinkle on the cheese if required and serve.**

An Eye For Good Food

# SPRING LAMB STEW

(Dr Helen Orton from Liverpool for the Foundation)

*Helen has provided us with a gluten free recipe for a hearty lamb stew. This recipe requires skinning tomatoes which is easily done if the tomatoes are put in hot water just off the boil and then the skin splits for easy peeling.*

**(Serves 6)**

15 ml (1tblsp) sunflower oil
6 lamb chops
15ml (1tblsp) cornflower
6 ripe tomatoes, skinned deseeded and chopped.
3 garlic cloves crushed
900ml (about 1 2/3rd pts) of lamb or chicken stock
2 bay leaves
3 or 4 sprigs of thyme
30ml (2tblsps) fresh chopped parsley
6 carrots cut into circles
500g (1lb+) of leeks washed and cut into similar size circles
300g ( 2/3rd lb) of sugar snap peas
300g ( 2/3rd lb) of mange tout
300g ( 2/3rd lb) of white baby turnips chopped

**Brown the chops for 2 mins on each side in oil heated in a large casserole dish then on lower heat add some salt and the flour and mix well. Now add in the tomatoes, stock, garlic, thyme and bay leaves. Bring to the boil then on reduced heat simmer covered by the lid for 45 mins. Skim off any foam and add carrots, leeks, turnip, half of the parsley and cook for a further 25 mins. Finally add in the sugar snaps and mange tout and they will only need 6 mins. Serve the stew up with new potatoes and sprinkle on the remaining parsley.**

An Eye For Good Food

# BOBOTIE

(Dr Helen Orton from Liverpool for the Foundation)

*Bobotie is South African scouse or maybe cottage pie. It tastes nothing like them but it is a dish that every South African mum makes in her own slightly different way and it is the essence of home cooking. Thank you Helen for this contribution – there are several South Africans who work at St Pauls and I'm sure they will give this bobotie recipe their seal of approval. One consultant and his wife run a well known South African restaurant in the Merseyside Cheshire region and bobotie is often on the menu.*

**(Serves 6)**

3 slices of white bread
3 onions chopped
15ml (1tblsp) of olive oil
2 cloves of garlic crushed
1kg (2.2lbs) of lean steak mince
10ml (2tsps) of Madras curry paste
5ml (1tsp) dried mixed herbs
5ml (1tsp) of ground cloves
2.5ml (½ tsp) all spice
45ml (3tblsps) mango chutney
60ml (4tblsps) of sultanas and chopped dried apricots
9 bay leaves

**FOR THE TOPPING**
275ml (½ pt) full cream milk
2 large eggs

**Pour cold water over the bread and let it soak and set the oven at 180°C. Then gently fry the chopped onion in oil for 10 mins until soft at that point add in the garlic and mince crushing and stirring the mince to break up any lumps and help browning. Stir in the curry paste, herbs, spices, chutney, dried fruits and 3 bay leaves, season and simmer with cover on for 10 mins. Taste and depending on what you like add more curry paste if you wish. Squeeze water out of bread and stir it into the meat mixture until it is well blended in. Tip the mixture into an oven proof dish and press it down so it is smooth on top.**

**Beat the eggs and milk together, season, pour the topping on the meat and scatter over the remaining bay leaves. Cover with foil and bake for 35-40 mins by which time the topping will have set and started to colour. Serve with salad and rice.**

An Eye For Good Food

**MAIN COURSES**

# PERSIAN STYLE LAMB WITH RHUBARB

(Dr Helen Orton from Liverpool for the Foundation)

*Rhubarb and lamb make such an interesting combination. Helen points out that if you have forced rhubarb or champagne rhubarb rather than the more usual standard stuff it needs less cooking.*

**(Enough for 6 to 8)**

45 ml (3 tblsps) of vegetable oil
125g (4oz) of butter
3 large sliced onions
2 crushed cloves of garlic
1 ½ Kg (3.3lbs) of diced shoulder of lamb
30ml (2 tblsps) ground coriander
1.2L (2pts) of vegetable stock (hot and best quality)
30g (1oz) of chopped fresh parsley
45g (1 ½ oz) of chopped fresh mint
600g (around 1 ¼ lbs) of rhubarb

**Heat the oil and around 40g of butter in a large casserole dish then add the onions and cook slowly for 15 mins then add in the garlic and cook some more (2 mins). Remove from the dish and then increase the heat and seal the lamb all over doing the meat in batches. Get all the meat and onions back in the dish and stir in the coriander. After a min introduce the stock cover and simmer for 1 hr. Meanwhile melt 45g of butter into a pan and cook the parsley and 30g of mint slowly for 10 mins. Add these to the casserole dish and continue cooking for a further 30 mins. While the casserole is cooking cut the rhubarb into 3 cm pieces, melt the rest of the butter in a pan and cook the rhubarb for at least 4 mins and up to 10 mins (unforced) until tender. Add the rhubarb to the lamb and cook a few mins more and serve this up on couscous (flavoured with lemon and coriander perhaps?) or rice and decorate the dish with the rest of the chopped mint.**

*An Eye For Good Food*

# LAMB COBBLER

(Margaret Guppy from Liverpool for Bradbury Fields)

*Margaret's cobbler rather than using scone mix uses a French loaf stick making it a little easier but still very tasty.*

**(Plenty for 4)**

675g (1 ½ lbs) of lean diced lamb
Seasoned flour to coat the meat
1 large chopped onion
2 chopped carrots
1 chopped stalk of celery
450ml ( ¾ pt) stock
15ml (1tblsp) tomato puree
2.5ml ( ½ tsp) dried rosemary
½ a French loaf
Butter for the bread

**Toss the chopped lamb in the flour and set aside. Heat the oil in a pan and cook the carrot, celery and onion over low heat until they begin to soften and this will take up to 5 mins. Remove with a slotted spoon and place in a 1.75L (3pt) casserole dish. Add the floured meat to the original pan and brown for 4 mins then add the meat to the casserole. Now add the stock to the pan with the tomato puree and the rosemary and when on the boil pour the liquid on the casserole. Cover the dish and cook at 180°C for 1 ¼ hrs. Slice the loaf and butter one side (garlic butter and dried herbs are an option). Place on top of the casserole and cook for up to 20 mins and serve at once.**

An Eye For Good Food

# STEAK & KIDNEY PIE

(Phil Welsh from Wavertree, Liverpool for the Foundation)

*Arguably the French have the best stews in the World but I believe that the British have by far the best pie recipes. Steak and kidney pie deserves to be at or near the top of the British pie hall of fame but too often it is a miserable cheap mass produced affair that comes from some bakery that could do much better or it is snatched from the freezer shelves of a supermarket chain where the picture on the packet is far better than the content. Many frozen pies are made of poor pastry and the content is brown goo and gristle. Now this is where home cooking comes into its own and shows us what a really good pie can be like. Thank you Phil your recipe raises the humble steak pie back to its rightful place at the top of the food chain!*

**(Serves up to 6)**

200g (7oz) plain flour
(seasoning)
700g (1 ½ lb) braising steak trimmed of fat and cubed
175g (6oz) ox kidney cored and chopped
100g (3 ½ oz) butter
1-2 garlic cloves skinned and crushed
1 large onion skinned and chopped up
100g (3 ½ oz) mushrooms
150ml (around ¼ pt) beef stock
150ml (around ¼ pt) brown ale
1 bay leaf
Sprig of fresh thyme or 2.5ml (½ tsp) dried thyme
15ml (1tblsp) Worcestershire sauce
15ml (1tblsp) tomato puree
Fresh milk for glazing

**Season 25g (1oz) of flour and then toss the steak and kidney pieces in the flour shaking off any excess. Melt 25g (1oz) of butter in a large saucepan and lightly fry the garlic, onion and mushrooms for 3 minutes. Add in the steak, kidney and any leftover coating flour and cook for 5 minutes. Then gradually stir in the stock and ale. Add in the bay leaf, thyme, Worcestershire sauce and tomato puree then cover and simmer for 1 ¼ hours. Spoon the mixture into a 1.7L (3pt) pie dish. Take the remaining flour, a little salt and rub the butter in until it resembles breadcrumbs. Add 4tblsp of cold water and mix to form a dough. Roll out on a lightly floured work surface to about 2 inches (5cm) wider than the pie dish. Cut a 1 inch (2.5cm) strip all round and brush the rim of the pie dish with water and stick on the pastry strip now brush this strip with water and cover the pie with the pastry lid crimping down at the rim pressing lightly to make an effective seal. Trim off any excess pastry and check your seal crimping where needed. Garnish with pastry leaves, make a couple of holes for steam and brush with milk and bake the pie at 200°C for at least 30 minutes up to 45 minutes.**

An Eye For Good Food

# TANGY SLOW COOKER POT ROAST

(Tom Southern from Wirral for the Foundation)

*In a busy household a slow cooker is a gem, Dee and I use ours all the time and it is great to get home after a long day to the wonderful smells of your dinner ready for you. Tom is in charge of fund raising for the Foundation and describes his recipe as "a flavourful pot roast of beef in a tangy mixture of wine and broth" – great let's get cooking!*

(Serves 8)

1 ½ kg (between 3 and 4lbs) of boneless beef chuck roast
10ml (2tsps) Hungarian paprika
Salt and pepper
30ml (2tblsps) olive oil
125ml (4oz) of beef stock or consume
125ml (4oz) of red wine (or more stock)
45ml (3 tblsps) balsamic vinegar
15ml (1tblsp) honey or brown sugar
1 can (250g) tomato sauce (passata)
1 large onion sliced
1 large carrot sliced
3 cloves of garlic thinly sliced

**Heat the oil in a skillet or frying pan, season the beef and rub in the paprika. Cook for about 5 minutes browning all over. Meanwhile combine the stock, wine, tomato sauce, vinegar and honey and set to one side. Put the onion, carrots and garlic into the bottom of the slow cooker and then add the beef on top. Pour the stock and wine mixture into the frying pan to soak up the browning and use a spatula to scrape off any residual brown bits and finally pour all of this into the slow cooker. Cover and cook on high for 4 ½ to 5 ½ hours or if you have the time after 1 hour reduce to low and allow 7 to 9 hours slow cooking. Serve with lots of creamy mash, green beans and corn for as Tom says "a delicious family meal".**

An Eye For Good Food

An Eye For Good Food

# Desserts

We have to thank Margaret Guppy and Dr Helen Orton particularly for most of our desserts. And great ones they are!

# BREAD & BUTTER PUDDING

(Margaret Guppy from Liverpool for Bradbury Fields)

*Bread and butter pudding is such a warming pudding but it, like many warming and filling puddings, seems to be out of favour these days. That is a real shame because it is a great British institution and perhaps through Margaret's recipe we can get to like it once again.*

(For 4)

3 slices of bread and butter with the crusts removed
60g (2oz) of mixed dried fruit
550ml (1 pt) of milk
1 egg
30g (1oz) caster sugar
1.25ml (¼ tsp) nutmeg

**Arrange the buttered bread and dried fruit in layers in a buttered oven proof dish. Warm the milk and pour it over the beaten egg and sugar. Let the pudding stand for an hour then sprinkle on the nutmeg and caster sugar. Place the dish in a roasting tin with a little hot water then in the oven and bake at 180° for about 30 minutes.**

# RICE PUDDING

(Margaret Guppy from Liverpool for Bradbury Fields)

*Margaret says "A homemade rice pudding can be delicious on a cold day" and who can argue with that?*

(Serves 4)

75g (3oz) short grain rice
35 to 40g (1 ½ oz) caster sugar
550ml (1pt) of milk
15ml (1tblsp) butter
2.5ml (½ tsp) of grated nutmeg

**Rinse the rice and place it in a buttered oven proof dish. Add the sugar and milk and stir. Bake in the middle of an oven at 140°C for 1 hour. Add the butter and nutmeg to the top of the pudding then give it 1 more hour in the oven, Margaret says to avoid stirring the pudding one stir at the beginning is enough.**

An Eye For Good Food

# CHOCOLATE SAUCE & FRUIT

(Keith Teare from Oxton, Wirral for the WSBPS)

*Keith makes these delicious chocolate dips and of course chocolate and strawberries are ideal partners for a tasty pudding.*

**(From 1 to 4 people)**

225g (8oz) of dark chocolate
150ml (¼ pt) of single cream
15ml (1tblsp) of caster or icing sugar
30ml (2tblsps) of amaretto liqueur
450g (1lb) of fresh hulled strawberries

**Break up the chocolate and place it in a bowl over simmering water, mix in the cream, sugar and the liqueur when the chocolate has started to melt. Keep the bowl warm on a hot plate and start dipping in the strawberries – enjoy!**


# ICE CREAM & FRUIT TART

(Dee Grierson)

*These tarts are easy to put together and are a real hit with adults and children alike. We make up one big tart for the children and individual small tarts for adults because the big dessert can be messy when you chop it up.*

**(Serves 6)**

225g (½ lb) plain biscuits
110g (around 4oz) unsalted butter
450g (1lb) frozen tropical fruit
1 lemon
15ml (1 tblsp) of icing sugar
1 tub (450g) of vanilla ice cream
2 chocolate flakes

**Crush the biscuits in a polythene bag and melt the butter and mix the two together in the butter pan. Then transfer the biscuit mix to a 23cm (9 inch) diameter baking tin and make sure the biscuit makes a base but also extends up the sides. Bake at 1900C for 30 mins to set the biscuit and then cool. Blitz the partly frozen tropical fruit with lemon juice and sugar and set aside. Fill the biscuit case with ice cream, pour on the fruit sauce and sprinkle with chocolate. Serve immediately or keep in freezer until needed – fine for a few weeks.**

# RHUBARB CRANACHAN

(Dr Helen Orton from Merseyside for the Foundation)

*Cranachan is a very Scottish dessert that the Grierson's usually have on Burns Night and the dish is usually based on raspberries so Helen's version which uses rhubarb is unusual to me but works well because the dessert needs a rather "tart" flavour to offset the cream.*

**(Enough for 8 people)**

1Kg (2.2lbs) of rhubarb
3 pieces of stem ginger finely chopped
The syrup from the stem ginger jar
125g (4oz) of sugar
90g (3oz) of rolled oats
90g (3oz) Demerara sugar
275ml (½ pt) double cream
275ml (½ pt) natural yoghurt

### PREPARE THE RHUBARB
**Preheat the oven to 180°C then wash and cut the rhubarb into 2.5cm pieces. Cut the stem ginger finely and place the rhubarb in an oven proof dish and sprinkle on the ginger, sugar and syrup from the jar. Bake in the oven until the rhubarb is soft (about 25 mins) and allow to cool.**

### PREPARE THE TOPPING
**Place the oats on a baking tray and toast under the grill for a few moments do not let the oats burn. Remove these and mix with the Demerara sugar. Whisk the cream until it thickens up and then add in the yoghurt. Put some rhubarb in a fluted glass, the cream mixture on top and a sprinkle of sugary, toasted oats on top. Enjoy!**

# STRAWBERRY & MINT FOOL

(Dr Helen Orton from Merseyside for the Foundation)

*Strawberries are always high in the lists of so called "super foods". The super food concept has more to do with marketing than nutrition although strawberries score highly in terms of nutritional value. All that is irrelevant as far as our young daughter Megan is concerned, she eats strawberries like other kids eat sweets. Megan does not respond to marketing or nutritional advice (from her Dad) - to her only one thing matters and that is that they taste delicious!*

(Serves 8)

675g (1 ½ lb) of strawberries washed and hulled
30g (1oz) of golden caster sugar
550ml (1pt) of double cream
275g ( ½pt) mascarpone cheese
30ml (2tblsps) of fresh chopped mint.
8 small sprigs of mint

**Reserve 8 strawberry halves and put the rest, the chopped mint and your sugar into a blender and blitz till smooth. Whip the cream and then add the mascarpone whisking in gently and making sure there are no lumps. Fold the fruit puree into the creamy cheese and then spoon into serving glasses and chill until needed. Serve up with s sprig of mint and half a strawberry on each pudding.**

An Eye For Good Food

DESSERTS

# BLACKBERRY MERINGUE

(Margaret Guppy from Liverpool for Bradbury Fields)

*Frozen or fresh, blackberries are just bursting with Vitamin C and they are such a wonderful autumn fruit don't you think?*

(For 6 or so)

675g (1 ½ lbs) of blackberries
Granular sugar to taste
4 egg whites
225g ( ½ lb) of icing sugar

If the blackberries are fresh they will need a rinse. Place them in an oven proof dish with enough granular sugar to suit your taste. Whisk the whites until stiff and then add icing sugar gradually. When all the sugar is added and the meringue is made, cover the fruit completely with the mixture and bake at 170°C of up to 40 minutes. Let the pudding cool and serve it chilled.


# ALMOND FRITTERS

(Margaret Guppy from Liverpool for Bradbury Fields)

*Margaret says these fritters can be eaten by people who are gluten intolerant. I think that the rest of us would enjoy one or two of them; particularly me because I cannot resist almonds in any shape or form.*

(Enough for 4)

2 eggs
30g (1oz) of caster sugar
60g (2oz) of ground almonds
2.5ml (½ tsp) of vanilla essence
12g (½ oz) of corn flour
A little olive oil

Separate the yolks of the eggs and beat them and the sugar together. Then add the almonds, vanilla essence, cornflour and the stiffly whisked egg whites. Put the oil in a frying pan and when hot drop in spoonfuls of the mixture cooking them until golden. Drain and serve warm.

An Eye For Good Food

# FRUIT JELLY

(Ian Grierson)

*I have to admit that I love jellies and here is a version that you can have at any time but will make a fine pudding to finish off a meal when you have guests.*

**(6 jellies)**

375ml (13fl oz) of grape juice
125ml (5fl oz) of sweet Valencia wine
1 packet (block) of fruit jelly (any flavour you like)
250g (9oz) mixed berries (frozen is fine)
120ml (¼ pt) of crème fraiche

**Break up the jelly and partly defrost the berries if needed. Warm the grape juice and add in the wine and all the jelly cubes letting the jelly dissolve. Put the berries into about six serving glasses (wine glasses are fine). Let the dessert set in the fridge and put some crème fraiche or whipped double cream on top before serving.**

# CHERRY SHERRY PANCAKES

(Terri Homes from Wirral for the WSBPS)

*Terri says make pancakes to your own recipe (or you might buy crepes from the baker or supermarket readymade if you like). Don't stint on the sherry and you know you have eaten enough when you can no longer say cherry sherry pancakes!*

**(2 per person to start with)**

Plenty of pre-prepared pancakes
1 large tin (400g +) of cherry pie filling
45ml (3tblsps) of sherry per pancake
1 tub (450g) of ice cream (or whipped cream)

**Spread each pancake with pie filling and roll them up and with two pancakes per plate give them 1 min in the microwave. Pour over your sherry and have a scoop of ice cream or cream on the side!**

92

# Chutneys & Drinks

Just a few things that we think are rather special to finish up with.

# MEDITERRANIAN CHUTNEY

(Jenney Borley from Wirral for the WSBPS)

*Jenny is the Centre Manager for the WSBPS and a magician in her spare time, I know this because she magics together amazing chutneys for most of the WSBPS functions. I am her greatest fan and this chutney is my favourite – no pork pie or slice of cheese is safe once I have my hands on a jar of Jenny's chutney.*

**(Enough for about 4 lb)**

1Kg (2.2lb) of tomatoes skinned and chopped
450g (1lb) of courgettes thinly sliced
1 large red pepper diced
450g (1lb) of chopped onion
1 large green pepper diced
225g (½ lb) of aubergine diced
2 garlic cloves
15ml (1tblsp) of Cayenne pepper
15ml (1tblsp) of Paprika
10ml (2tsps) of salt
275ml (½ pt) of malt vinegar
15ml (1tblsp) of ground coriander
185g (6ozs) of sugar

**Place the tomatoes, onions, courgettes, peppers, aubergines and chopped garlic into a large pan. Add all the condiments and cover and cook gently until the juices run. Then bring to the boil, reduce heat, uncover and simmer for up to 1 ½ hours or until the vegetables are soft but still keeping their shape. Most of the tomato water will have gone. Add the vinegar and sugar stirring until all the sugar is dissolved. Cook for a further hour until the chutney is thick and there is no free vinegar on top. Spoon the mixture when it is still hot into sterile jars and seal with airtight vinegar proof lids. It should mature in 6 months.**

# JAR-MADE TOMATO RELISH

(Ian Grierson)

*It isn't really a relish, more a jar of this and that and although it does not sound promising it is absolutely delicious with cheese. I'm sure it will last OK in the fridge but to be honest we never have it around long enough. It is high in antioxidants and has none of the sugar issues associated with most relishes and chutneys.*

**(At least 2 medium sized jars)**

Jar (250-300g) of sun dried tomatoes
Jar (250-300g) of mixed mushrooms
A jar (100g) of anchovy fillets
3 spring onions
5ml (1tsp) chilli flakes

**Drain the 3 jars into a food processor reserving some of the liquid and add in the spring onions and chilli. Blitz but leave the mixture still with plenty of texture then mix in some of the reserved oils from the jars. Fill a couple of jars with the mixture and reserve or use immediately with your favourite cheese and strips of toasted pita bread.**

# SANGRIA MIXTURE

(Ian Grierson)

*There are all sorts of variations on the Sangria theme even in Spain the mixture is extremely inconsistent however the basic elements are a bottle of red wine, a variable amount of lemonade, lots of ice, lots of fruit, at least one shot of hard liquor and lots of good holiday spirit! Here is the sangria recipe I usually make.*

**(6 to 8 drinks)**

1 (75ml) bottle of red wine
1L bottle of lemonade
10ml (2tsps) frozen vodka
1 lemon
1 orange
1 apple
15ml (1tblsp) sugar
Plenty of ice

**Put lots of ice and all the sliced fruit into a jug that has been cooled in the fridge. Take a bottle of red wine (chilled) and the litre of lemonade plus the chilled vodka and add to the jug and stir in the sugar.**

*An Eye For Good Food*

# LEMONADE

(The Grierson Family)

*We make home-made lemonade on a regular basis. OK there is a lot of sugar in the recipe but there is also fruit juice in abundance. In line with our home cooking theme we have a lot of fun making this lemonade.*

**(Makes about 10 drinks or so)**

1L (1 ¾ pts) of water
5ml (1tsp) powdered ginger
300g (10 ½ oz) of sugar
6 organic lemons

**Heat the water in a pan and add the sugar and ginger letting the sugar dissolve. Grate in the rind of 4 of the lemons and juice all 6 adding these to the hot liquid. Let the lemonade cool and keep in the fridge overnight. Next day filter into a jug and it will keep for up to 5 days in the fridge. It dilutes about 50/50 with shop lemonade for the kids and with tonic or soda water for us.**

# TOMATO CHUTNEY

(Jenny Borley from Wirral for the WSBPS)

*Jenny recently went to Hawaii on holiday and was sorely missed – for a start we had to live without her chutney for a few weeks. Tomatoes have an important health micronutrient called lycopene which, because it is lock into the walls of the tomatoes it is hard to release – making the tomato into chutney should do it however!*

**(Again about 4 lbs of chutney in the recipe)**

1kg (2.2lbs) of tomatoes skinned and sliced
225g (½ lb) of apples peeled and cored
225g (½ lb) of sultanas
225g (½ lb) of chopped onions
225g (½ lb) of sugar
275ml (½ pt) of malt vinegar

5ml (1tsp) pickling spice
5ml (1tsp) mustard powder
2.5ml (½ tsp) powdered ginger
2.5ml (½ tsp) salt
A generous 1ml (¼ tsp) pepper

**Put the pickling spice into a little piece of muslin. Put the onion into a pan with 3tblsps of vinegar and simmer gently until nearly soft and add the chopped apples, skinned tomatoes, spices, salt, pepper, mustard, ginger and sultanas. Simmer until all the mixture is quite soft stirring from time to time. Add the remainder of the vinegar and the sugar making sure the sugar dissolves and then boil steadily until the chutney is like jam. Remove the spice bag, pour the chutney into warm sterile jars and seal immediately.**

# PEPPER RELISH

(Grierson Family)

*The red pepper relish has no added sugar and can be eaten hot or cold. The relish is full of antioxidants but we make it because it has a lovely flavour and reminds us of a great family holiday in Sardinia. It brings us a memory of hot weather that is sorely lacking in the UK these days.*

**(One medium sized jar)**

3 cloves of garlic
3 red peppers
4 tomatoes
30ml (2tblsps) of chilli infused olive oil (or just add 1tsp of chilli powder/flakes to normal olive oil)
1 (350g) jar of primavera (or good quality chopped tomato with herbs)
(Seasoning)

Deseed and chop up the peppers into thin strips and slice the garlic. Fry both in the chilli oil for around 4 mins. Chop up the tomatoes and add them and the primavera and heat through for a further 5 mins plus. The mixture can be eaten hot with fried eggs or any meat or on toast. If not needed immediately put it into a sterile jar with a good lid and it will keep for a couple of weeks. As a cold relish it goes well with burgers or any barbeque food.


# CHEESE & PINEAPPLE MIXTURE

(Dave Evans from Morton, Wirral for the WSBPS)

*Dave says this is nice to make up for a barbeque or something to have with savoury biscuits for supper.*

**(Plenty for 6 to 8, but don't run out of biscuits)**

140g (5oz) of cream cheese
140g (5oz) of cottage cheese
250g tin of pineapple chunks
2.5ml ( ½ tsp) ground cinnamon
2.5ml ( ½ tsp) powdered ginger

Drain the pineapple, add a little of the juice and the cheeses and spice to a food processor and blitz until smooth. Store in the fridge until needed but best to be eaten the same day.

An Eye For Good Food

# **A Few Last Words**

I hope you enjoyed the book and found some interesting recipes. We want to thank all those who submitted recipes and we wish good fortune and every success in the fabulous work they do to the 3 charities that have been involved in this project.